NADIA LIM'S
GOOD FOOD COOK BOOK

NADIA LIM'S
GOOD
FOOD
COOK
BOOK

*Simple, healthy & delicious
food for busy people*

RANDOM HOUSE
NEW ZEALAND

A RANDOM HOUSE BOOK published by
Random House New Zealand
18 Poland Road, Glenfield, Auckland,
New Zealand

For more information about our titles
go to www.randomhouse.co.nz

A catalogue record for this book is available
from the National Library of New Zealand

Random House New Zealand is part of the
Random House Group
New York   London   Sydney   Auckland
Delhi   Johannesburg

First published 2013

© 2013 text Nadia Lim, photography Tamara West

The moral rights of the author have been asserted

ISBN 978 1 77553 506 5

Design: Strategy Design & Advertising
Photography: Tamara West
Props: Tamara West and factoryceramics.co.nz
Printed in China by Everbest Printing Co. Ltd

For Carlos — thank you for coming along the journey with me. Here's cheers to lots of laughs, stories, great food and wine around the table!

8   good food

16   breakfasts

42   lunches

70   entrées, snacks & side dishes

100   dinners

      102   vegetarian

      124   fish

      144   poultry

      168   meat

196   lighter desserts

228   treats & home baking

248   essentials

254   acknowledgements

256   index

good food

By good food, I mean food that is both delicious and nutritious. As a cook and dietitian it's equally important to me that food tastes great and is just as good for you. I've created these delicious and simple recipes with a focus on lots of colourful seasonal vegetables and fruit, healthy grains and nourishing protein so they're packed full of goodness that will look after you and your body. I want you to get off to a great start every day with a nutritious breakfast, look forward to a tasty and hassle-free lunch, and have fun cooking up and serving delicious, healthy dinners the whole family will love. I want you to get excited about cooking, eating and sharing good food every day!

The key to a healthy diet is to eat a wide variety of unprocessed 'real food': food that has been refined or processed as little as possible, leaving it packed full of nutrients just as nature intended. Enjoy food from the ground, the sea and the sky — and avoid highly processed food from the factory — and you will be on the right track towards healthier eating. The guidelines on the following pages will help you with this.

I like to emphasise what we should be eating, instead of what we shouldn't be — if you focus on getting all the servings of fruit, vegetables, grains and protein you need every day, there is little room for eating less nutritious foods. A positive approach to eating will help develop healthy habits that last a lifetime. For example, instead of saying that you won't snack on biscuits when you're hungry, say you will snack on a piece of fruit. This approach will liberate you from being controlled by numbers if you're trying to lose weight; instead your new healthy habits will naturally result in weight loss.

In this book, you'll find meals for throughout the day, from breakfast and brunch through to lunch, snacks, entrées and dinner. Treats are one of life's greatest pleasures and (in moderation) can fit into a healthy diet, so rest assured I've included a whole section on tempting desserts, too! I've put a lighter twist on many of them so you won't break the calorie bank by having pudding. Then there are the more occasional indulgences and baking; as while I believe in having things in moderation, sometimes it doesn't hurt to enjoy moderation in moderation, too!

Last but not least, how you eat is just as important as what you eat. Eating slowly, having a relaxed attitude towards food and being mindful of the food's journey to your plate are all important factors that will help you cultivate a healthier relationship with food, and at the same time you'll enjoy your food more. Good food enjoyed around the table with family and friends truly is the best medicine, as strong as any remedy out there. So enjoy cooking, eating and sharing these yummy recipes with the knowledge that what you're eating is good for you, too!

Eat at least 5 serves of vegetables a day

If there is any one food group you can't eat too much of it's vegetables. Vegetables are rich in antioxidants, vitamins, minerals and fibre and the bonus is they're low in calories. The wider the variety of vegetables (and colours) you eat, the wider the range of antioxidants (protective compounds) you'll get; each colour is representative of different antioxidants — for example, red and orange indicates the presence of carotenoids, and dark green vegetables are high in folate. The biggest vegetable eaters are also the healthiest, with the lowest risk of any nutrition-related diseases. So eat as many vegetables as you can over the day, including them in lunch, dinner and even breakfast and snacks.

Eat at least 2–3 serves of fruit a day

Fruit is nature's original sweet treat and is packed full of soluble fibre, vitamins, minerals and antioxidants. You needn't worry about the (naturally occurring fructose) sugar content of fruit — unless you are eating a bucketful in one sitting — its high fibre content slows down the rate of sugar absorption. Eating in season means the fruit will be fresher, tastier and more nutritious because it has been picked and delivered at ripeness, instead of being kept in cold storage for long periods where nutrients degrade. Fruit is the best healthy snack available – it's quick, portable, cheap and good for you. So if you want a snack in between meals, make sure it comes from a tree, and not the vending machine!

Eat breakfast every day

Eating breakfast is one of the most important habits associated with long-term health and weight control, and improved academic performance in children. Yet it is the meal most likely to be skipped. Missing breakfast makes you more prone to snacking or binge-eating later on in the day, which can result in the calories stacking up fast. For an ideal breakfast that will keep you going until lunch, include some low-glycaemic-index (GI) carbohydrates, some milk, yoghurt or other alternative for protein and calcium, and some fruit, and, even better, vegetables! — a fruit and vegetable juice in the morning is a great boost to your vitamin and mineral intake. If you're in a rush you can have your breakfast 'to go'. I've provided some quick ideas and recipes for breakfasts you can take with you as you head out the door.

Serve yourself the right portions and follow the plate model

Over the years portion sizes have increased significantly, which has added to our weight issues. Everyone's calorie needs are different and portion sizes should reflect this. Use your hand as a good guide — serve yourself a 'fist' of carbohydrates, a 'palm' of protein, and at least a whole hand of vegetables. Remember one person's hand will differ to the next person's, a man's from a woman's and an adult's from a child's. To get the balance right, the majority of my main meals follow the 'plate model', with at least half vegetables, roughly one-quarter carbohydrates, one-quarter protein and a small amount of fats and sugars. This is a good guide to go by on an everyday basis to ensure you meet your recommended servings of all the food groups. These meals average about 550 calories per serve, which is perfect for a main meal in a healthy balanced diet.

Eat unprocessed, wholegrain carbohydrates

Carbohydrates that have been minimally processed, or not at all, tend to be much higher in fibre, nutrients and have a lower glycaemic index (GI). This means you have more stable blood-sugar levels throughout the day because the glucose from the carbohydrates is released more slowly than in processed foods – this is because the body takes longer to digest and absorb wholegrains. You do the processing instead of the factories doing it for you. Opt for natural unprocessed carbohydrates such as root vegetables and legumes (e.g. beans, chickpeas and lentils) which are high in fibre, vitamins and minerals, and have no additives.

Eat healthy fats

Fat is an essential part of a healthy diet, playing a huge role in heart health, mood and even controlling weight. For a while fat was blamed for our health issues, resulting in an obsession with low-fat foods and diets — unfortunately this was to the detriment of our health (many low-fat products are highly processed and not any better for you). More than the amount, the *type* of fat you eat is important. You're on the right track if you can lower the amount of saturated fat, which is linked to high cholesterol, in your diet. Healthy monounsaturated and polyunsaturated fats found in avocados, nuts, seeds and oily fish protect your heart and support overall health. With all the fat-soluble vitamins (vitamins A, D, E and K) that come in these foods, your skin and hair will love you for it, too.

Treat yourself occasionally

A happy and healthy relationship with food is one where you don't feel guilty about having treat foods every now and again. Worrying too much about being healthy isn't good for anyone's health; after all, it's how you eat most of the time that matters, not the occasional over-indulgence. As a rule of thumb, aim to eat well 90 per cent of the time, and feel free to enjoy being a little more indulgent 10 per cent of the time.

A delicious balanced week

	Monday	Tuesday	Wednesday
BREAKFAST	**Nourishing breakfast:** Creamy rice porridge (page 32) with ½ cup vanilla and orange marinated tamarillos (page 40)	**Breakfast on the run:** Huevos rancheros-style breakfast pita pocket (page 22)	**Smoothie breakfast:** Avocado and raspberry smoothie (page 30)
SNACK	3 crackers with coriander hummus (page 68)	Fruit	Small handful of fruit and nut mix
LUNCH	**Lunch with leftovers:** Peanut, coriander and chicken vermicelli noodle salad (page 48)	**Vegetable-packed lunch:** Tamari-roast pumpkin, chickpea and walnut salad (page 60)	**Quick-and-easy lunch:** Smoked chicken, avocado and mango salad (page 46)
SNACK	Chia seed pudding (page 38)	Banana smoothie	Fruit
DINNER	**Meat-free Monday night:** Eggplant, portobello mushroom and mozzarella free-form lasagne (page 112)	**15-minute meal:** Salmon tom yum (page 126)	**Fun kid's night:** Cajun fish tacos with mango salsa and chipotle sour cream (page 132)
AFTER DINNER	Black Doris plum sorbet (page 208)		Fruit salad

Thursday	Friday	Saturday	Sunday
Antioxidant-hit breakfast: Purple juice (page 36)	**Friday morning breakfast meeting:** 2 super breakfast muffins (page 18)	**Relaxed weekend breakfast:** Tropical fruit muesli (page 20) with home-made yoghurt (page 28) and milk	**Sunday brunch with friends:** Hot Texas-style hash 'n' eggs (page 24)
Chia seed pudding (page 38)			
		Green juice (page 37)	
Fruit	Fruit		
Warming lunch: Butternut satay soup (page 55)	**Packed lunch in the park:** Smoked salmon niçoise salad (page 63)	**Light lunch:** Prawn, watermelon, tamarind and coconut salad (page 56)	**Healthy nibbles platter:** Mint and feta yoghurt dip with crisp baby vegetables (page 72)
			Creamy mango ice-block (page 219)
Casual pizza night: Lebanese lamb pizza with carrot salad (page 188)	**Dinner to impress:** Roast tomato, thyme and goat's cheese crostini (page 74)	**Healthy weekend barbecue:** Barbecue prawns with spicy mango and chilli dipping sauce (page 90)	**Sunday roast night with a twist:** Roast chicken, Jerusalem artichokes, bacon, Brussels sprouts and gravy (page 166)
	Beef tataki with apple and radish (page 82)		
	Five-spice duck, pomegranate glaze, kumara mash and sesame spinach (page 152)	Barbecued lamb and olive panzanella (page 174)	
Banana choc-chip ice-cream (see page 209)	Coconut vanilla yoghurt panna cotta with marinated berries (page 222)	Turkish rose pavlova (page 244)	

breakfasts

Breakfast is the meal most likely to be skipped. For many people it's the time factor — not being a morning person myself (and wanting to get every last minute of sleep!) I can sympathise with this. To make sure I always have a good breakfast, even if I'm running out the door, I have quick ready-made breakfasts handy — my super-breakfast muffins are perfect for those rushed mornings. Others don't feel very hungry first thing, especially if they have to get up early — in these cases a fruit smoothie, such as my avocado and raspberry smoothie, is a great way to have something nutritious and delicious that's easy to stomach.

I probably don't need to tell you that eating breakfast every day is one of the most important habits linked to weight control in adults and concentration in children. So to adopt the long-term habit of breakfast every day, you have to enjoy it and look forward to it — which means avoiding the boredom of having the same breakfast over and over again (unless you want to!). It's a good idea to vary your breakfasts throughout the week and different seasons, keeping them fun and delicious — having 'pudding' for breakfast, like my creamy rice porridge, or leftover fruit crumble, is a surefire way to get you eating in the morning!

Aim to have one to two servings of fruit, one to two servings of complex carbohydrates (oats, rice, potato, wholegrain toast) and a serving of protein (eggs, milk, yoghurt) at breakfast, which will keep you going until lunch time. There's lots of potential to include vegetables at breakfast too — have some wilted spinach, mushrooms or tomato and you'll be one or two vegetable servings up for the day.

In this section you'll find a mixture of faster convenient breakfasts for busy weekdays and a few fun, more generous ones for the weekend; they are all are sure to get you off to a great start to the day.

Super Breakfast Muffins

These muffins are packed full of fibre and freeze well. They make a great 'breakfast to go' on those mornings you don't have time to prepare breakfast from scratch — just warm one up in the microwave. Make sure you don't over-mix the batter — this will ensure the muffins stay light and tender.

MAKES: 12 MEDIUM MUFFINS

PREP TIME: 15–20 MINUTES

COOK TIME: 20 MINUTES

dates 1 cup chopped
water ½ cup
baking soda 1 teaspoon
butter 50g, softened
brown sugar 1 cup
vanilla extract or **essence** 1 teaspoon
egg 1, beaten
bananas 2 very ripe, mashed
carrot 1 loosely packed cup grated
walnuts or **other nuts** 1 cup chopped
wholemeal flour 1 ½ cups
bran ½ cup
baking powder 1 teaspoon
ground mixed spice ½ teaspoon

FREEZES WELL   VEG

Per serve
Energy: 1047kj (250 cal)
Carbohydrate: 33.8g
Protein: 5.7g
Fat: 10.3g
Saturated fat: 3.0g

1 Preheat oven to 180°C. Lightly grease and line a 12-hole muffin pan with paper cases. Place dates and water in a small saucepan and boil for about 5 minutes, stirring frequently to mash up the dates. Add baking soda and mix well — it will froth up a bit.

2 Beat butter with brown sugar and vanilla until thick, light and creamy, then beat in egg. Mix in mashed banana, grated carrot, nuts and date mash.

3 Stir flour, bran, baking powder and mixed spice together. Add to wet mixture and fold the two mixtures together with a large metal spoon, until well combined. Do not over-mix.

4 Spoon batter into lined muffin pans. Bake for 20 minutes or until muffins spring back when lightly touched.

Tropical Fruit Muesli

Making your own muesli is easy, quick and will save on your grocery bill. It is also much healthier than most of the pre-packaged cereals in fancy boxes, which are often high in added sodium and sugar. To make the muesli gluten-free, use 5 cups of puffed quinoa and rice instead of the oats.

1 Preheat oven to 170°C. Line an oven tray with baking paper. Combine oil, honey, ginger, cardamom or cinnamon and salt in a medium-sized saucepan and melt over low heat. Stir in rolled oats.

2 Scatter rolled oats over prepared oven tray and bake for 15 minutes until starting to go a light golden brown.

3 Remove from oven and allow to cool completely before tossing with coconut, nuts and dried fruit. Store in an airtight container in a cool, dark place. It will keep for a couple of months.

MAKES: 7 CUPS

SERVES: 14

PREP TIME: 10 MINUTES

COOK TIME: 15 MINUTES

neutral or nut oil (e.g. canola, soy or rice bran) 3 tablespoons
honey ¼ cup
ground ginger ½ teaspoon
ground cardamom or **cinnamon** ½ teaspoon
salt pinch of
large rolled oats 3 cups
thread coconut or **coconut chips** ¾ cup
macadamia or **Brazil nuts** 1 cup chopped
dried tropical fruit (e.g. dried mango, papaya, pawpaw, pineapple) 1½ cups, chopped
dried apricots ½ cup chopped

Per serve
Energy: 1086kj (259 cal)
Carbohydrate: 27.9g
Protein: 4.5g
Fat: 14.6g
Saturated fat: 5.0g

Breakfast Pita Pockets

You can whip up these breakfast pita pockets in less than 5 minutes for a yummy breakfast that's easy to hold in one hand while you head out the door. They're bound to get you off to a good start!

SERVES: 1

PREP TIME: 3–5 MINUTES

COOK TIME: 2 MINUTES

1 For the herb, spinach, egg and ham version, mix eggs with parsley, cheese and baby spinach, and season with salt and pepper. Either scramble in the microwave, or on the stove top (see below for methods). For the huevos rancheros version, simply season eggs and scramble as below.

2 To scramble eggs in the microwave, place beaten eggs and a small knob of butter in a bowl and microwave for 45 seconds to 1 minute on high, then whisk with a fork and microwave for a further 30 seconds.

3 To scramble on the stove top, melt butter in a small frypan on medium heat and add beaten eggs. Use a spatula or wooden spoon to move eggs around the pan while they cook, 1–2 minutes.

4 Warm pita pocket quickly in the microwave for 15–20 seconds. Cut 2cm off the top (so there is an opening), and stuff with ham and scrambled eggs, or avocado, tomato, salsa, coriander and scrambled eggs.

Tip I prefer my eggs soft and ever so slightly runny, but it's up to you how firm you want them.

HERB, SPINACH, EGG AND HAM

eggs 2, beaten
parsley 2–3 tablespoons chopped
cheese 2 tablespoons grated
baby spinach handful
butter knob of
salt
black pepper freshly ground
wholemeal pita pocket 1 medium (10–12cm diameter)
ham 1 slice

Per serve
Energy: 1660kj (397 cal)
Carbohydrate: 22.1g
Protein: 30.9g
Fat: 20.8g
Saturated fat: 9.6g

HUEVOS RANCHEROS

salt
black pepper freshly ground
eggs 2, beaten
butter knob of
wholemeal pita pocket 1 medium (10–12cm diameter)
avocado 3 slices
tomato 1 small, sliced
tomato salsa 1½ tablespoons
coriander 2 tablespoons chopped

(Use oil instead of butter)

Per serve
Energy: 1544kj (369 cal)
Carbohydrate: 25.8g
Protein: 19.7g
Fat: 20.6g
Saturated fat: 3.8g

Hash 'n' Eggs

This is one of those dishes that triples as a breakfast, lunch or easy dinner and can make use of a multitude of different leftovers (e.g. sliced sausages or steak) and spices (try curry powder or harissa). The eggs are cooked in the potato mixture, making it a one-pot meal.

SERVES: 2

PREP TIME: 10 MINUTES

COOK TIME: 20–25 MINUTES

HOT TEXAS-STYLE HASH 'N' EGGS

Agria potatoes 2 medium, scrubbed and cut into 2.5cm cubes
olive oil 1 tablespoon
onion 1 small, diced
streaky bacon 2 rashers, diced
cayenne pepper ¼ teaspoon
ground cumin ¼ teaspoon
eggs 2
lemon juice of ½
chipotle or **hot sauce** 1 tablespoon
natural unsweetened thick Greek yoghurt ¼ cup
salt and **black pepper** freshly ground
coriander ½ cup chopped

1 Cook potatoes in boiling salted water until just tender, about 10 minutes. Drain and set aside.

2 Heat olive oil in a heavy-based medium frypan on medium heat and cook onion, bacon, cayenne pepper and cumin if making Hot Texas-style hash, or onion, chorizo, capsicum and paprika if making Spanish-style hash, until onion is soft, 3–4 minutes. Add cooked potatoes and a drizzle of oil; fry potatoes, breaking them up slightly with a wooden spoon. Continue frying for 4–5 minutes until the bottom of the potatoes starts to crisp up.

Per serve
Energy: 1409kj (336 cal)
Carbohydrate: 34.8g
Protein: 14.8g
Fat: 19.1g
Saturated fat: 5.7g

GLUTEN FREE

SPANISH-STYLE HASH 'N' EGGS

3 Make two 'holes' or indents in the potato mixture and carefully crack an egg into each cavity. Squeeze over lemon juice and place a lid or plate on top (the juice will help create steam to cook the eggs). Cook, covered, for 3–4 minutes for runny yolks, or 2–3 minutes longer if you prefer a firmer yolk.

4 Mix chipotle or hot sauce with Greek yoghurt for Hot Texas hash 'n' eggs.

5 Turn off the heat, season eggs with salt and pepper, dollop over chipotle yoghurt if using and garnish with coriander or flat-leaf parsley depending which version you are making. To serve, use a large spoon to carefully place some potato hash and an egg onto each plate.

Agria potatoes 2 medium, scrubbed and cut into 2.5cm cubes
olive oil 1 tablespoon
red onion 1 small, diced
firm chorizo sausage ½, diced or sliced
red capsicum 1, diced
smoked paprika 1 teaspoon
eggs 2
lemon juice of ½
salt and **black pepper** freshly ground
flat-leaf parsley ¼ cup chopped

Tip Boiling the potatoes before cooking them in the pan ensures they 'crush' easily and mingle with all the different flavours.

Per serve
Energy: 1510kj (360 cal)
Carbohydrate: 33.2g
Protein: 15.6g
Fat: 18.6g
Saturated fat: 4.6g

DAIRY FREE   GLUTEN FREE

(Use gluten-free chorizo)

Home-made Yoghurt

Yoghurt has a 100 per cent yield from milk, meaning that the amount of milk you use is the amount of yoghurt you'll end up with, which makes it very economical. All you need is milk, a couple of tablespoons of plain yoghurt to provide live cultures (good bacteria) for fermentation and a warm place to keep the cultures happy — a hot water cupboard is ideal.

1 Place milk in a pot and bring to a gentle boil before turning off the heat. Allow milk to cool for 10 minutes or until it reaches 45–50°C (test with a thermometer). At this stage whisk in yoghurt.

2 Pour into a Thermos flask, large glass jar or plastic container, cover and wrap in a tea towel. Leave in a warm place overnight (e.g. the hot water cupboard).

3 After about 8 hours you will have fresh yoghurt. If it is grainy, whisk until smooth. Use and flavour as you like — see right for some suggestions.

Tip If the yoghurt is too runny for your liking, drain in a sieve lined with clean paper towels or muslin cloth, over a bowl in the fridge (covered) for a few hours or until the desired thickness is reached. The watery whey will drip out.

MAKES: 1 LITRE

PREP TIME: 15 MINUTES

STANDING TIME: 8 HOURS

milk standard full-fat 1 litre
natural unsweetened yoghurt
   3 tablespoons

PLUM AND CINNAMON

Mash or purée together the flesh of 4 canned Black Doris plums, 2 teaspoons plum jam and ¼ teaspoon ground cinnamon. Stir through fresh yoghurt.

APRICOT, HONEY AND ORANGE BLOSSOM

Mash or purée together the flesh of 10 canned apricot halves, 3 teaspoons honey and 2 teaspoons orange blossom water (optional). Stir through fresh yoghurt.

PASSIONFRUIT

Stir ⅓ cup passionfruit syrup (see page 253) through fresh yoghurt.

GLUTEN FREE

Per serve
Energy: 350kj (83 cal)
Carbohydrate: 6.0g
Protein: 4.5g
Fat: 4.7g
Saturated fat: 2.9g

Avocado *and* Raspberry Smoothie

Avocados are considered the most nutritious fruit in the world because they contain such a vast array of vitamins and minerals, as well as protein and healthy monounsaturated fats. Adding avocado makes a really thick, creamy, filling smoothie that is full of goodness.

raspberries frozen, 1½–2 cups
avocado 1 firm ripe, chopped
banana 1
milk or **yoghurt** 1½ cups
runny honey 1–2 tablespoons

(Dairy free with soy or almond milk)

Per serve
Energy: 1676kj (400 cal)
Carbohydrate: 36.8g
Protein: 12.1g
Fat: 23.2g
Saturated fat: 3.3g

1 Blend everything together in a blender or food processor until smooth. Pour into glasses and serve.

Creamy Rice Porridge

Similar to rice pudding, this makes a great gluten-free alternative to oat porridge. Commonly eaten for dessert, rice pudding makes a great nutritious breakfast, too. Serve with vanilla and orange marinated tamarillos (page 40) or with fresh or canned fruit for a delicious, sustaining breakfast high in calcium.

1 Preheat oven to 160°C. In a large casserole or Pyrex dish, combine all ingredients and stir.

2 Cook for 1½ hours, stirring a few times during the cooking to break up the skin that forms on top.
To serve, spoon some creamy rice porridge into a bowl and top with fresh or canned fruit (e.g. plums, peaches, apricots) or vanilla and orange marinated tamarillos (see page 40).

Tip The rice pudding will keep in the fridge for up to a week and can be served warm or cold. To warm it up, add a few tablespoons of milk to loosen, stir, then warm in the microwave.

SERVES: 6

PREP TIME: 5 MINUTES

COOK TIME: 1½ HOURS

short- or **medium-grain rice**
   6 tablespoons
milk 5½ cups
orange finely grated zest of 1 (optional)
nutmeg freshly grated, ½ teaspoon
ground cinnamon ¼ teaspoon
vanilla extract or **essence** 1 teaspoon
sugar 3 tablespoons
honey 2 tablespoons

(DAIRY FREE) (GLUTEN FREE) (VEG)

(Dairy free with soy or almond milk)

Per serve
Energy: 271kj (65 cal)
Carbohydrate: 32.5g
Protein: 9.2g
Fat: 3.7g
Saturated fat: 2.2g

Rainbow Juices

Juice is a great way to get some antioxidants, and bump up your fruit and vegetable count for the day.

Yellow Juice
(Pineapple, Carrot *and* Ginger)

Chop and juice ½ fresh pineapple (skin off), 2 large carrots and 2.5cm piece ginger.

Per serve
Energy: 329kj (78 cal)
Carbohydrate: 31.3g
Protein: 1.7g
Fat: 0.8g
Saturated fat: 0.1g

Purple Juice
(Beetroot, Orange, Apple *and* Lemon)

Chop and juice 1 large beetroot, 2 oranges (skin off), 1 green apple and 1 lemon (skin off).

Per serve
Energy: 292kj (70 cal)
Carbohydrate: 22.3g
Protein: 2.4g
Fat: 0.9g
Saturated fat: 0.2g

Green Juice
(Apple, Spinach, Carrot *and* Orange)

Chop and juice 2 green apples, 2 large handfuls baby spinach, 1 large carrot and 1 orange (skin off).

Per serve
Energy: 425kj (102 cal)
Carbohydrate: 20.8g
Protein: 2.0g
Fat: 1.2g
Saturated fat: 0.3g

Thick Red Juice
(Raspberry, Strawberry *and* Cranberry)

Place ½ cup fresh or frozen raspberries, ½ cup fresh or frozen strawberries and 1 cup cranberry juice in a blender or food processor and process until smooth.

Per serve
Energy: 250kj (60 cal)
Carbohydrate: 11.8g
Protein: 1.5g
Fat: 0.8g
Saturated fat: 0.05g

Chia Seed Pudding

Chia seeds come from the flowering plant *Salvia hispanica*, commonly known as 'chia', which is native to Mexico. Like other seeds, they are very high in fibre. Chia seeds are also a great plant source of omega 3. When mixed with liquid, they take on a gel-like texture, making them popular for puddings, smoothies and breakfasts.

1   Mix everything together in a bowl or pouring jug. Stir for 2 minutes until mixture begins to thicken.

2   Pour into 3 or 4 small bowls or serving glasses, dividing mixture equally. Place in fridge for at least 3 hours or overnight to thicken. Serve with fruit for breakfast or pudding.

SERVES: 3–4

PREP TIME: 5 MINUTES

CHILLING TIME: 3 HOURS

chia seeds ½ cup
milk 2 cups
maple syrup ¼ cup, or **runny honey** 3 tablespoons
vanilla bean paste or **vanilla extract** or **essence** 1 teaspoon

DAIRY FREE   GLUTEN FREE   VEG

(Dairy free with soy or almond milk)

Per serve
Energy: 763kj (182 cal)
Carbohydrate: 26.5g
Protein: 9.0g
Fat: 9.0g
Saturated fat: 1.2g

Vanilla *and* Orange Marinated Tamarillos

After marinating for a couple of hours, the tamarillos form their own syrup that is flavoured with the vanilla and orange, making them a divine dessert, or breakfast.

SERVES: 4

PREP TIME: 5 MINUTES

MARINATING TIME: 2 HOURS

tamarillos scooped-out flesh of 10–12
vanilla bean paste 1 teaspoon,
    or **vanilla bean pod** seeds of 1
orange juice of 1
sugar 2 tablespoons

DAIRY FREE   GLUTEN FREE   VEG

Per serve
Energy: 221kj (53 cal)
Carbohydrate: 10.2g
Protein: 2.1g
Fat: 0.4g
Saturated fat: 0.07g

1 Place tamarillos in a non-corrosive bowl and gently mix with vanilla, orange juice and sugar.

2 Cover and leave in fridge for at least 2 hours or overnight to marinate and form its own syrup. Serve cold or warmed up with porridge, cereal or semolina.

lunches

Lunch provides the energy to keep you mentally focused and to sustain you throughout the afternoon by keeping your blood sugar levels stable. Without it, you'll probably find you lack energy and concentration or, worse, become 'hangry' (hungry-angry)!

During the work week, bringing a packed lunch will save your dollars and waistline by providing an alternative to the vending machine, fast-food chain or greasy work canteen (which will only leave you feeling tired and sluggish). But you don't want to get to your well-deserved break after a busy morning, only to face the disappointment of the same old soggy sandwiches or limp salad either! A little creative use of common pantry staples and last night's leftovers will avoid this.

I like to base lunch around at least two servings of vegetables, one serving of complex carbohydrates (lentils, beans, chickpeas, root vegetables, noodles, pasta, rice, etc) for long-lasting energy, a serving of protein (egg or a bit of cheese or meat) and some healthy fats (avocado, nuts, seeds) to keep me going until late afternoon or dinner time.

Many of these recipes make use of common leftovers such as cooked potato, noodles, pasta, chicken and steak. Throw them together with a sauce or dressing that is full of flavour, a big handful of vegetables and a sprinkling of nuts or seeds, and you've got a lunch that will make you the envy of your colleagues!

It requires only a little organisation. Pack your lunch the night before but keep all the components separate in your lunchbox, ready to toss together for a freshly made meal, to avoid the soggy version. Or, in colder weather, make up a batch of soup and freeze individual portions for an easy lunch you just have to heat up.

Roast Carrot, Parsnip, Herb *and* Feta Puy Lentil Salad

Puy lentils hold their shape when cooked, making them ideal for salads. Like other legumes, lentils have a very low glycaemic index, so will keep you full for longer (and ensure more stable blood sugar levels). This makes an excellent healthy packed lunch.

SERVES: 2–3

PREP TIME: 10–15 MINUTES

COOK TIME: 20–25 MINUTES

baby carrots 1 bunch, trimmed and peeled
parsnips 2, peeled and cut into sticks
runny honey 1 tablespoon
olive oil 1 tablespoon
salt
black pepper freshly ground
dried Puy lentils ½ cup
feta 50–60g, crumbled
medjool dates 4, chopped
flat-leaf parsley ½ cup chopped
fresh oregano or **marjoram** ¼ cup chopped (optional)
dukkah 2 tablespoons
extra virgin olive oil 1–2 tablespoons
lemon juice of ½

GLUTEN FREE   VEG

Per serve
Energy: 1138kj (272 cal)
Carbohydrate: 35.8g
Protein: 17.5g
Fat: 6.6g
Saturated fat: 3.8g

1 Preheat oven to 200°C. Line an oven tray with baking paper. Bring a small saucepan of water to the boil for the lentils. Halve any longer carrots lengthways. Lay carrots and parsnips on prepared oven tray. Drizzle and toss with honey and olive oil and season with salt and pepper. Roast for 20–25 minutes until soft and caramelised.

2 While vegetables are roasting, cook lentils in boiling water until just tender but still with a bit of bite (about 20 minutes). Drain and set aside.

3 Toss roast vegetables with lentils, feta, dates, herbs and dukkah. Season to taste with salt and pepper. Dress with extra virgin olive oil and lemon juice just before serving.

Tip Make sure you boil the lentils in unsalted water — salted water will toughen them.

Smoked Chicken, Avocado *and* Mango Salad

This super-tasty meal is more than quick to make. If taking as a packed lunch or planning to serve later, keep the tossed salad and dressing in separate containers and only toss together just before serving to avoid the vegetables wilting.

SERVES: 4

PREP TIME: 10–15 MINUTES

basil sweet chilli dressing ½ cup (see page 253)
mango 1 ripe, peeled and sliced
cherry tomatoes 1 punnet, halved
telegraph cucumber ½, halved lengthways and sliced
red onion 1 small or ½ medium, thinly sliced
avocado 1 firm ripe, sliced
basil leaves handful
salad leaves 4 handfuls
smoked chicken breasts 2, sliced
garlic bread or **foccacia loaf** 4 slices, toasted and cut into fingers, to serve

(Gluten free without bread)

Per serve
Energy: 1596kj (381 cal)
Carbohydrate: 26.7g
Protein: 18.2g
Fat: 21.9g
Saturated fat: 4.7g

1. Toss dressing with mango, cherry tomatoes, cucumber, red onion, avocado, basil, salad leaves and chicken. Divide salad between plates and serve with garlic bread or foccacia.

Peanut, Coriander *and* Chicken Vermicelli Noodle Salad

This is an easy toss-together salad that is full of fresh and aromatic Asian flavours. It's a great way to use up leftover cooked chicken, steak or prawns. See method on page 59 for poaching chicken breasts.

1 Combine all dressing ingredients.

2 Place noodles in a large bowl or medium-sized saucepan and pour over boiling water. Cover and stand for 5 minutes until noodles are soft. Drain and rinse under cold water to prevent sticking together. Use scissors to snip noodles in a few places (to shorten their length).

3 Toss noodles with dressing and all remaining ingredients. Divide between serving bowls.

Tip If taking as a packed lunch or planning to serve later, keep tossed salad and dressing in separate containers and only toss together just before serving to avoid vegetables wilting.

SERVES: 4–5

PREP TIME: 15 MINUTES

DRESSING

sweet chilli sauce 6 tablespoons
fish or **soy sauce** 1½ tablespoons
sesame oil 1½ tablespoons
oil (e.g. canola, soy or rice bran) 1½ tablespoons
lime juice ¼ cup
hoisin sauce 2 teaspoons

SALAD

dried vermicelli noodles (glass noodles) 100g
roast chicken shredded meat of ½, or **poached chicken breasts**, shredded meat of 2
coriander 1½ cups chopped
red onion 1 small or ½ medium, thinly sliced
purple cabbage 2 cups finely shredded
Lebanese cucumbers 2, peeled into ribbons with a vegetable peeler
kaffir lime leaves 2, central stem removed and finely chopped
red chilli 1, chopped (optional)
roasted peanuts or **cashew nuts** ½ cup chopped

DAIRY FREE

Per serve
Energy: 1792kj (429 cal)
Carbohydrate: 33.2g
Protein: 24.1g
Fat: 22.1g
Saturated fat: 4.0g

Raw Rainbow Salad

After eating this antioxidant-packed salad you'll feel fresh, healthy and revitalised. Raw beetroot is delicious with its sweet and earthy flavours. Serve with thin slices of raw salmon sashimi to make it into a light main meal.

SERVES: 4–6

PREP TIME: 15 MINUTES

carrots 2 large, shredded or grated
beetroot 1 large, peeled and shredded or grated
spring onions 2, thinly sliced
purple cabbage 1 cup finely shredded
shallot 1, finely diced
cherry tomatoes ½ punnet, halved
mint leaves ¼ cup sliced
coriander leaves ¼ cup chopped
lime and sesame dressing ½ cup (see page 252)
alfafa sprouts 2 handfuls
pumpkin and/or **sunflower seeds** small handful

1 Toss carrots, beetroot, spring onion, cabbage, shallot, tomatoes and herbs together in a large bowl. Pour dressing over and toss together gently.

2 Divide salad between bowls and top with alfafa sprouts and pumpkin and/or sunflower seeds.

DAIRY FREE · GLUTEN FREE · VEG

Per serve
Energy: 574kj (137 cal)
Carbohydrate: 6.8g
Protein: 3.4g
Fat: 10.9g
Saturated fat: 1.5g

Creamy Roast Capsicum Soup *with* Parmesan Croutons

Roast capsicums have a sweet, very subtle smoky flavour and are incredibly useful for stews, salads, pizzas and dips, or in this delicious velvety summer soup. Roasting until the capsicums are blackened, charred and blistered intensifies their flavour and makes the skins easy to peel off.

SERVES: 2–3

PREP TIME: 10 MINUTES

COOK TIME: 30–40 MINUTES

ROAST CAPSICUM SOUP

red capsicums 7–8 large
red chilli 1 large (optional)
olive oil 1 tablespoon
onion 1, diced
garlic 2 cloves, chopped
ground coriander ½ teaspoon
ground cumin ½ teaspoon
tomato paste 1½ tablespoons
vegetable or **chicken stock** 1 cup
crème fraîche 3 tablespoons
lemon juice of ½
salt
black pepper freshly ground

PARMESAN CROUTONS

ciabatta or **sourdough bread** 3 slices, roughly cut into 2cm cubes
olive oil 1 tablespoon
parmesan cheese ½ cup grated

TO SERVE

crème fraîche 3 tablespoons (optional)
coriander or **flat-leaf parsley** ¼ cup chopped

FREEZES WELL   GLUTEN FREE   VEG

(Gluten free without croutons)

Per serve
Energy: 1402 kj (335 cal)
Carbohydrate: 25.3g
Protein: 13.5g
Fat: 20.4g
Saturated fat: 7.9g

1   Preheat oven to 220°C. Place whole capsicums on an oven tray and roast for 20–25 minutes until skins are blackened, charred and blistered. Halfway through cooking time, add chilli if using and roast until skins are charred and blistered. Allow capsicums and chilli to cool slightly before peeling off skins — the skins should come off quickly and easily. Split in half and discard seeds of capsicums and chilli (or keep chilli seeds if you would like some heat in the soup). Roughly chop.

2   Lower oven temperature to 200°C. Heat olive oil in a small frypan on medium heat. Cook onion, garlic, coriander and cumin until onion is soft, 4–5 minutes. Add tomato paste and cook for a further minute.

3   Place capsicum and chilli flesh, onion mixture, vegetable or chicken stock, crème fraîche and lemon juice in a blender or food processor. Blend until smooth. Transfer soup to a saucepan and heat through. Season to taste with salt and pepper.

4   To make the croutons, toss bread cubes with olive oil and parmesan. Place on a baking tray and bake for 5–10 minutes or until crisp and golden.

5   To serve, divide soup between bowls and top with a dollop of crème fraîche if using, some chopped herbs and parmesan croutons.

Butternut Satay Soup

Butternut makes the most delicious soup. This one is jazzed up with some spices and chilli, as well as a secret ingredient — peanut butter! — which gives the soup a subtle satay flavour that is really delicious.

SERVES: 4–6

PREP TIME: 10 MINUTES

COOK TIME: 25 MINUTES

olive oil 2 tablespoons
onions 2 large, chopped
garlic 3 cloves, chopped
ground cumin 1 teaspoon
ground coriander 1 teaspoon
curry powder 1 teaspoon
chilli flakes good pinch
tomato paste 1½ tablespoons
butternut 1.3–1.4kg (skin off), chopped
  into 3cm chunks
chicken stock 1.25 litres
smooth peanut butter 4–5 tablespoons
lemon juice 1–2 tablespoons
salt
black pepper freshly ground
natural unsweetened Greek yoghurt
  ½ cup (optional)
coriander ¼ cup chopped to garnish
red chilli 1 large chopped to garnish
  (optional)

(Dairy free without yoghurt)

Per serve
Energy: 1366kj (326 cal)
Carbohydrate: 27.5g
Protein: 12.1g
Fat: 15.5g
Saturated fat: 3.4g

1 Heat olive oil in a large saucepan on medium heat. Cook onions and garlic for 5 minutes until onion is soft. Add spices and chilli flakes and fry for a few minutes, then add tomato paste and fry for a further minute. Add a little water at any time if onions or spices are sticking to the bottom of the pan. Add butternut and chicken stock. Bring to the boil, lower heat and cook until butternut is soft, about 15 minutes.

2 Transfer to a food processor along with peanut butter. Blend until smooth. Season to taste with lemon juice, salt and pepper. (If you have used stock made from stock powder the soup may not need salt.)

3 Divide soup between bowls and garnish with a dollop of yoghurt if using, and chopped coriander and chilli if using.

Prawn, Watermelon, Tamarind *and* Coconut Salad

This salad is full of refreshing and aromatic flavours, perfect for an entrée or light meal — especially in summer when watermelon is sweet and juicy. The sharp and sour flavours of lime and tamarind make this a nice dressing for Asian-style salads.

1 Combine all dressing ingredients and set dressing aside.

2 Heat oil in a wok or large frypan on high heat. Add prawns and garlic, and stir-fry for 2–3 minutes until prawns are just cooked. Season with salt.

3 Toss prawns, watermelon, avocado, cucumber, mint, coriander and toasted coconut with dressing just before serving.

* **Tip** Make tamarind water by mixing ¼ cup water with 1 tablespoon tamarind concentrate, or ½ cup boiling water with 1 tablespoon tamarind pulp, and straining.

** **Tip** Toast coconut in a dry frypan on medium heat for 1 minute until light golden, moving frequently so it doesn't burn.

SERVES: 4

PREP TIME: 20 MINUTES

COOK TIME: 5 MINUTES

DRESSING

tamarind water* ¼ cup
ginger ½ teaspoon, minced
brown sugar 1½ teaspoons
kaffir lime leaves 2, central stem removed, finely chopped
lime juice of 2
red chilli 1, finely chopped (optional)
fish or **soy sauce** 2 teaspoons

SALAD

oil (e.g. canola, soy or rice bran) 2 tablespoons
prawn cutlets 16–20 large, shelled with tails left on
garlic 2 cloves, minced
salt
watermelon 3 cups chunks
avocado 1 firm ripe, sliced
Lebanese cucumber 1, diced
mint leaves ½ cup, torn
coriander ½ cup roughly chopped
toasted thread coconut** ¼ cup

(Use gluten-free soy sauce)

Per serve
Energy: 1335kj (319 cal)
Carbohydrate: 10.6g
Protein: 17.9g
Fat: 22.6g
Saturated fat: 5.5g

Poached Chicken, Crouton *and* Bean Salad *with* Creamy Tarragon Dressing

This is like a much healthier version of a Caesar salad. Poaching is a great way to cook chicken without adding any fat. The key to it staying moist and juicy is not to overcook it — as soon as the liquid comes to a gentle boil, turn off the heat and cover; the chicken breasts will be cooked through in 10–15 minutes, depending on their size. The tarragon adds a lovely subtle anise flavour.

SERVES: 4

PREP TIME: 20 MINUTES

COOK TIME: 15 MINUTES

chicken breasts 2 boneless, skinless
tarragon 2 stalks
salt
olive oil 3 tablespoons
sourdough bread 6 slices, cut into 3cm chunks
green beans 200g, trimmed

DRESSING

butter 2 tablespoons
shallot 1, finely diced
garlic 1 clove, minced
tarragon leaves 2 tablespoons chopped
mayonnaise 2 tablespoons
natural unsweetened yoghurt 3 tablespoons
Dijon mustard 1 teaspoon
lemon juice of ½
salt
black pepper freshly ground

TO ASSEMBLE

cos lettuce ½ large, chopped
cherry tomatoes 1 punnet, cut in half

Per serve
Energy: 1892kj (452 cal)
Carbohydrate: 28.9g
Protein: 27.6g
Fat: 25.9g
Saturated fat: 8.0g

1. Place chicken breasts and tarragon stalks in a small saucepan and cover with cold water so that the chicken breasts are fully submerged. Add a good pinch of salt and bring to a gentle boil. As soon as it boils, turn off heat, cover and leave for 10–15 minutes until chicken is just cooked through (you can check by cutting it with a sharp knife).

2. Remove chicken from liquid and, when cool enough to handle, shred meat.

3. While the chicken is poaching, make the croutons. Heat olive oil in a large frypan on medium heat and cook bread chunks for 3–4 minutes until golden and crispy, tossing frequently. Season with salt and set aside.

4. Place green beans in a bowl and pour over boiling water. Stand for 2–3 minutes before draining and running under cold water.

5. To make the dressing, melt butter in a small saucepan and gently sauté shallot and garlic until soft, about 2 minutes. Stir in tarragon leaves, then turn off the heat. Mix with mayonnaise, yoghurt, Dijon mustard and lemon juice and season to taste with salt and pepper.

6. Lightly toss dressing with shredded chicken, beans, lettuce, tomatoes and half the croutons. To serve, divide salad between plates and garnish with remaining croutons.

Tamari-roast Pumpkin, Chickpea *and* Walnut Salad

Tamari is a wheat-free dark Japanese soy sauce. Pumpkin or butternut is delicious tossed with a drizzle of tamari and honey, then roasted until dark and caramelised. Serve as a side dish with some almonds scattered on top, or make the full recipe for a yummy, healthy and filling salad packed with fibre, vitamins and minerals.

SERVES: 4

PREP TIME: 10 MINUTES

COOK TIME: 15–20 MINUTES

pumpkin or **butternut** 500g, cut into 2cm cubes
olive oil 1 tablespoon
sesame oil 1 teaspoon
tamari soy sauce 1 tablespoon
runny honey or **maple syrup** 1 tablespoon
salt
chickpeas 1 x 400g can, rinsed and drained
cherry tomatoes 1 punnet, cut in half
walnuts ¼ cup roughly chopped
baby rocket, **spinach** or **mesclun salad leaves** 4 handfuls
lemon juice to dress
extra virgin olive oil to dress

CORIANDER YOGHURT

natural unsweetened yoghurt ½ cup
coriander ¼ cup chopped

DAIRY FREE   GLUTEN FREE   VEG

(Dairy free without yoghurt)

Per serve
Energy: 1270.5kj (303.3 cal)
Carbohydrate: 27.8g
Protein: 11.5g
Fat: 12.5g
Saturated fat: 1.2g

1   Preheat oven to 200°C. Line an oven tray with baking paper. Lay pumpkin or butternut on prepared tray and drizzle with olive oil, sesame oil, tamari soy sauce and honey or maple syrup. Toss to coat well. Roast for 15–20 minutes until pumpkin or butternut is soft and caramelised. Season with a little salt to taste, if needed.

2   Toss with all remaining ingredients and dress with lemon juice and extra virgin olive oil just before serving. Mix yoghurt and coriander together and dollop over salad to serve.

Smoky Avocado, Corn, Capsicum *and* Egg Potato Salad

A really tasty potato salad with a creamy yoghurt and mayonnaise dressing that makes a great dish to take to a barbecue or for lunch.

SERVES: 4

PREP TIME: 10–15 MINUTES

COOK TIME: 10 MINUTES

waxy baby potatoes 800g, quartered
corn cobs 3, husks removed, cut in half
mayonnaise ¼ cup
natural unsweetened thick Greek yoghurt ¼ cup
smoked paprika 1 teaspoon
lemon juice of 1
salt
black pepper freshly ground
roast red capsicums 2, sliced (from a jar or make your own, see page 54)
avocado 1 firm ripe, cut into chunks
hard-boiled eggs 4, shelled and roughly chopped
red onion ½ small, thinly sliced
basil leaves 1 cup, torn

Per serve
Energy: 2247kj (536 cal)
Carbohydrate: 47.8g
Protein: 17.3g
Fat: 30.6g
Saturated fat: 6.0g

1 Bring a large-sized saucepan of salted water to the boil. Cook potatoes in boiling salted water until tender, about 10 minutes. Halfway through, add corn cobs in with potatoes. Drain potatoes and corn and allow to cool. Cut corn kernels off cobs when cool enough to handle.

2 Mix mayonnaise, yoghurt, smoked paprika and lemon juice together. Toss with potatoes and season to taste with salt and pepper.

3 Mix capsicum strips, corn kernels, avocado, egg and red onion together and lightly toss with potatoes. Garnish with basil leaves just before serving.

Smoked Salmon Niçoise Salad

I've put a spin on this classic dish with smoked salmon instead of tuna and the addition of dill and capers. This is a lovely lunch to make using leftover potatoes, just toss with all the other ingredients. It's impressive enough to serve as a special lunch, but convenient enough to take as a packed lunch that will make you the envy of the work lunchroom!

SERVES: 4–5

PREP TIME: 15 MINUTES

COOK TIME: 12 MINUTES

waxy baby potatoes 800g, halved or quartered to roughly the same size
salt
green beans 300g, trimmed
eggs 4

DRESSING

Dijon or **wholegrain mustard** 2 teaspoons
lemon juice of 1
extra virgin olive oil 4 tablespoons
fresh dill 3 tablespoons chopped
capers 2 tablespoons, roughly chopped
flat-leaf parsley ¼ cup chopped
black pepper freshly ground

TO ASSEMBLE

cherry tomatoes 1 punnet, cut in half
kalamata olives ½ cup
red onion 1 small or ½ medium, thinly sliced
hot-smoked salmon 400g, flaked into bite-sized pieces

1 Bring a medium-sized saucepan of water seasoned with 1 teaspoon of salt to the boil. Boil potatoes for 10–12 minutes until just tender (use the tip of a sharp knife to test if done). Drop beans into boiling water with potatoes and cook for a further 3 minutes. Drain potatoes and beans. Set aside.

2 Soft-boil eggs by placing eggs in a small pan of water, bring to the boil and cook for 4 minutes. (Time carefully!) Run eggs under cold water to stop the cooking process. Once cool, peel off shells.

3 In a large bowl (big enough to hold the salad), whisk all dressing ingredients together, seasoning with salt and pepper. Toss potatoes, beans, tomatoes, olives and red onion with the dressing.

4 To serve, divide salad between plates and top with flakes of salmon. Cut boiled eggs in half lengthways (the yolk should be ever so slightly runny) and place two halves on top of each salad.

Per serve
Energy: 2213kj (529 cal)
Carbohydrate: 35.6g
Protein: 33.3g
Fat: 28.6g
Saturated fat: 5.0g

Japanese Beef *and* Crunchy Vegetable Soba Noodles

This quick meal simply involves cooking noodles, stir-frying strips of marinated beef and serving with a tasty dressing and crisp raw vegetables for lots of texture. Soba noodles made purely from buckwheat are gluten-free.

SERVES: 4–5

PREP TIME: 10 MINUTES

COOK TIME: 10 MINUTES

BEEF

ginger 2.5cm piece, minced or grated
garlic 2 cloves, minced
soy sauce 2 tablespoons
runny honey or **brown sugar** 1 teaspoon
beef sirloin steak 500g, trimmed of excess fat, thinly sliced
peanut or other **oil** (e.g. canola, soy or rice bran) 2 tablespoons

VEGETABLES AND SOBA NOODLES

purple cabbage ¼, finely shredded
dried buckwheat soba noodles 300–350g
soy and hoisin dressing ½ cup (see page 252)
radishes 4–5 small, thinly sliced
celery 2 stalks, thinly sliced
spring onions 3, thinly sliced

DAIRY FREE

Per serve
Energy: 1710kj (408 cal)
Carbohydrate: 43.0g
Protein: 31.1g
Fat: 13.0g
Saturated fat: 3.6g

1   Combine ginger, garlic, soy sauce, honey or brown sugar and sliced beef in a bowl. Set aside to marinate for 10 minutes at room temperature while you prep the vegetables.Bring a large-sized saucepan of water to a boil.

2   Heat 1 tablespoon of the oil in a large wok or frypan on high heat until almost smoking. Add half of the marinated beef; stir-fry for 2–3 minutes until cooked through, then set aside. Repeat with remaining oil and beef. (Cooking the beef in two batches prevents the meat from stewing.)

3   Add shredded cabbage to the pan the beef was cooked in and quickly stir-fry for 1–2 minutes to soften slightly. Set aside.

4   Cook noodles in boiling water until just cooked (do not overcook), about 4 minutes. Drain and toss noodles with the soy and hoisin dressing.

5   To serve, divide noodles, cabbage and beef between bowls. Top with slices of radish, celery and spring onion.

Mezze Trio of Dips

These dips, using fresh herbs, spices, legumes and roast vegetables, are healthy and delicious. With warm pita bread they make a great lunch or snack.

SERVES: 6–8

MAKES: 2 CUPS OF EACH DIP

PREP TIME: 10–15 MINUTES

COOK TIME: 25–30 MINUTES TO ROAST THE BEETROOT

Coriander Hummus

Drain a 390g can of chickpeas. Blitz in a food processor with 1 tablespoon tahini paste, a large bunch of coriander (leaves and stems), roughly chopped, 1 chopped garlic clove, the juice of 1 lemon and 3 tablespoons extra virgin olive oil until well combined. Season with salt and pepper to taste.

DAIRY FREE GLUTEN FREE

(Gluten free without bread)

Per serve
Energy: 420kj (100 cal)
Carbohydrate: 7.0g
Protein: 3.4g
Fat: 5.6g
Saturated fat: 0.7g

Sundried Tomato Bean Dip

Drain a 400g can of cannellini beans. Blitz in a food processor with a roasted red capsicum (from a jar or roast your own, see page 54), ¼ cup chopped sundried tomatoes, 1 chopped garlic clove and ½ teaspoon smoked paprika until well combined. Season with salt and pepper to taste.

DAIRY FREE GLUTEN FREE

(Gluten free without bread)

Per serve
Energy: 235kj (56 cal)
Carbohydrate: 8.4g
Protein: 3.6g
Fat: 1.4g
Saturated fat: 0g

Beetroot, Mint *and* Yoghurt Dip

Preheat oven to 180°C. Peel 2 medium
beetroot and cut into 2cm-thick wedges.
Drizzle and toss with olive oil and maple
syrup. Roast for 25–30 minutes until soft
and caramelised. Leave to cool in the fridge.
Blitz cold beetroot with the juice of 1 lemon,
1 chopped garlic clove, 1 teaspoon each
fennel, coriander and cumin seeds and 1 cup
mint leaves. Add ⅓ cup natural unsweetened
thick Greek yoghurt and pulse in a food
processor a few times until just combined.
Season with salt and freshly ground black
pepper to taste.

To serve

Either serve dips on individual plates,
or in bowls as part of a shared meal. Drizzle
over some extra virgin olive oil and sprinkle
over 2–3 tablespoons toasted pumpkin seeds,
2–3 tablespoons dukkah or za'atar and
3 tablespoons chopped parsley. Serve with
warm or toasted pita bread or other fresh bread.

(Gluten free without bread)

Per serve
Energy: 135kj (32 cal)
Carbohydrate: 3.0g
Protein: 1.3g
Fat: 1.6g
Saturated fat: 0.9g

entrées, snacks & side dishes

I love holding dinner parties for friends and family — it's a great way to get everyone together for a fun evening in the comfort of your own home where you can eat and drink what you like (and for a much lower price). I'm all for doing three or four courses, but pick recipes that can be prepared in advance, so when it comes to serving, it's more assembly than cooking.

A cold entrée like my beef tataki or Thai marinated fish, a main where most of the meal just has to be reheated, and a dessert that can be made well in advance is the way to go. Shared platters, like my lemongrass and chilli chicken lettuce cups, are another great idea – food that people can have fun assembling themselves is always a hit.

While everyone else may be relaxed, the host can sometimes be a bit overwhelmed — I've experienced this plenty of times before. Talking to your guests while trying not to burn the meal and making sure everyone's drinks are topped up can be quite a juggle. The key to a stress-free dinner party is preparation and to feel in control (or at least appear that way even if you're a bit nervous). This will make your guests feel relaxed, which will have a flow-on effect back to you.

While I don't believe that eating in moderation need apply when it's a special occasion, the recipes in this section are still all healthy, with lots of fresh ingredients which won't leave you or your guests feeling weighed down before the main course, and you'll have room for dessert! Most of them can be prepared in advance to ensure that you spend less time in the kitchen, and more time enjoying yourself with your guests.

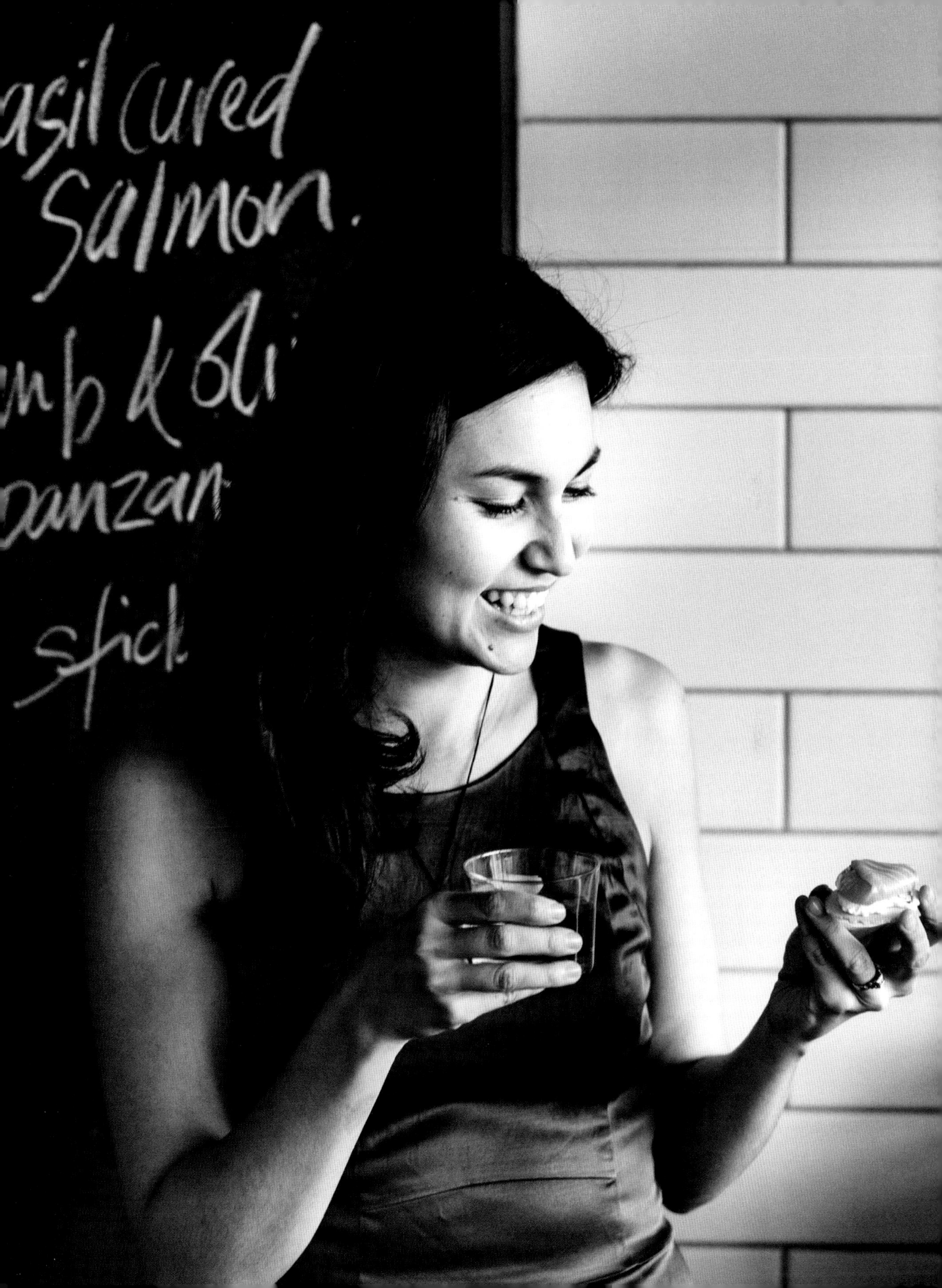
asil cured
Salmon.

Mint *and* Feta Yoghurt Dip *with* Crisp Baby Vegetables

This dip makes eating a big bowl of raw crisp vegetables a delight! Use any fresh vegetables you like, depending on the season – raw cauliflower florets, fennel and cucumber sticks make good 'dippers', too.

1 Bring a saucepan of salted water to the boil. To make the dip, blitz mint leaves in a food processor with lemon juice and avocado or extra virign olive oil. Add feta and Greek yoghurt and blitz until smooth. Season to taste with salt and pepper. Transfer to a bowl and mix through dill, if using.

2 Fill a bowl with ice and cold water. Blanch asparagus by plunging into boiling water for 30 seconds, then draining and plunging into iced water until ready to serve. This will ensure it retains its bright green colour and crunch.

3 To serve, arrange vegetables on a platter with a bowl of the dip on the side.

Tip The dip will keep for a few days in the fridge and is extremely handy as a dressing for salads or an accompaniment to meat, rice and couscous dishes. You can also add a chopped avocado to the food processor to make it an avocado, mint and feta yoghurt dip.

SERVES: 4 AS A CASUAL STARTER OR NIBBLE

PREP TIME: 5-10 MINUTES

MINT AND FETA YOGHURT DIP

mint leaves (stalks removed) 2 packed cups, roughly chopped
lemon juice of 1
avocado or **extra virgin olive oil** 2 tablespoons
feta 100g
natural unsweetened thick Greek yoghurt 1 cup
salt
black pepper freshly ground
fresh dill ½ cup chopped (optional)

BABY VEGETABLES

asparagus 8 spears, trimmed
baby radishes 6, quartered lengthways
baby carrots 12, trimmed and peeled
baby cos lettuce leaves 12
celery 2 stalks, cut into batons
snow beans 8, cut in half, or **sugar snaps** or **snow peas** 12

GLUTEN FREE   VEG

Per serve
Energy: 994kj (237 cal)
Carbohydrate: 8.8g
Protein: 9.6g
Fat: 18.1g
Saturated fat: 8.5g

Roast Tomato, Thyme *and* Goat's Cheese Crostini

Slow-roasting tomatoes intensifies their flavour and natural sweetness. Unlike other fresh fruit and vegetables, tomatoes improve nutritionally when cooked, increasing their lycopene antioxidant content. They are incredibly handy little flavour boosters tossed through salads, pasta or risotto, or as delightful little canapés like in this recipe.

1 Preheat oven to 120°C. Line an oven tray with baking paper.

2 Lay tomatoes, cut side up, on prepared oven tray. Drizzle with olive oil and season with salt. Cook for 1 hour 45 minutes until tomatoes are shrivelled (but they will still be juicy).

3 Carefully transfer tomatoes to a bowl. Add extra virgin olive oil, balsamic glaze, chopped thyme leaves and a pinch of salt. Gently toss together so as not to break the tomatoes.

4 To serve, spread some goat's cheese onto each crostini, and top with three tomato halves. Garnish with a few thyme leaves.

* Tip Balsamic glaze is a thick, sweet balsamic vinegar. You can find it at all gourmet food stores and some supermarkets. If you can't get it, make a substitute by boiling ½ cup of ordinary balsamic vinegar with 1½ tablespoons of brown sugar in a small saucepan for 4–5 minutes until thick and syrupy. Allow to cool before using.

** Tip You can buy pre-made crostini at gourmet food stores and supermarkets; however, you can make your own by cutting out small (roughly 2.5–5cm) rounds or squares from slices of sourdough or ciabatta bread. Brush with olive oil and bake in an oven preheated to 180°C for 10–15 minutes until crisp and golden.

SERVES: 8 AS A CANAPÉ

PREP TIME: 20 MINUTES

COOK TIME: 1 HOUR 45 MINUTES TO SLOW-ROAST

red cherry tomatoes 1 punnet, cut in half
yellow cherry tomatoes 1 punnet, cut in half
olive oil to drizzle
salt
extra virgin olive oil 1½ tablespoons
balsamic glaze* 2 tablespoons
thyme leaves 2 tablespoons chopped + extra to garnish
soft goat's cheese 100g (at room temperature)
crostini** 24–32 pieces

Per serve
Energy: 503kj (120 cal)
Carbohydrate: 8.8g
Protein: 4.8g
Fat: 7.4g
Saturated fat: 2.5g

Thai Salmon Cakes *with* Cucumber *and* Basil Chilli Mayo

I've eaten many fish cakes in my time and these are the best. They are delicious with fresh salmon, but are equally nice with fresh white fish. These cakes make very popular canapés — they'll be gulped up by your guests in a flash! You can fry them in advance and keep them in the fridge, then crisp them up in a hot oven just before serving.

SERVES: 6 AS A CANAPÉ

PREP TIME: 25–30 MINUTES

COOK TIME: 15 MINUTES

SALMON CAKES

fresh salmon fillet 450g (skin off), pin-boned and cut into cubes
ground cumin ¼ teaspoon
ground chilli powder ½ teaspoon
ground coriander ¼ teaspoon
brown sugar ½ teaspoon
kaffir lime leaves 2 large or 3 small, central stem removed and very finely chopped
ginger 1.5cm piece, chopped
garlic 2 cloves, chopped
coconut cream 3 tablespoons
fish sauce 2 tablespoons
red chilli 1, chopped
spring onions 3, chopped
panko crumbs 1–1½ cups
oil (e.g. canola, soy or rice bran) ¼ cup

BASIL CHILLI MAYO

Japanese mayonnaise ⅓ cup
sweet chilli sauce 2 tablespoons
basil leaves 20, chopped

TO SERVE

Lebanese cucumber 1, thinly sliced
red chilli 1, finely chopped
lime 1, cut into wedges to serve

1 To make the salmon cakes, place all ingredients, except panko crumbs and oil, in a food processor and pulse a few times until just combined to a thick paste.

2 Roll heaped teaspoons of mixture into balls (you will get about 24). Place panko crumbs on a plate and roll balls in crumbs to coat well. Lightly flatten each ball to form a mini patty shape.

3 Heat 1–2 tablespoons of the oil in a large frypan (preferably non-stick) on medium heat and cook salmon cakes in batches for 1–2 minutes on each side or until golden brown. Add more oil as required.

4 To make the mayo, mix all ingredients together.

5 Top each salmon cake with a slice of cucumber and a dollop of mayo. Sprinkle over red chilli. Serve on a platter with lime wedges to squeeze over just before eating.

DAIRY FREE

Per serve
Energy: 1770.8kj (422.9 cal)
Carbohydrate: 10.6g
Protein: 15.4g
Fat: 35.8g
Saturated fat: 7.9g

Salmon Sashimi *with* Ponzu

My favourite sashimi (raw fish) is salmon — delicious simply served with soy sauce and wasabi. However, this ponzu sauce with sharp and salty flavours is really good with it, too.

1 Toss ponzu dressing with carrot and radish and leave to marinate for 5 minutes while you prepare the salmon.

2 Use a very sharp knife to slice the salmon thinly. Arrange salmon on plates and top with marinated vegetables and dressing. Garnish with coriander and spring onion, and serve with Japanese pickled ginger and wasabi.

SERVES: 4

PREP TIME: 15 MINUTES

ponzu dressing ½ cup
carrot 1, peeled and shredded or cut into fine matchsticks
radishes 2 small, thinly sliced and cut into matchsticks
salmon fillet 250–300g (skin off), pin-boned
coriander leaves to garnish
spring onion shredded to garnish
Japanese pickled ginger to serve
wasabi to serve

DAIRY FREE   GLUTEN FREE

(Use gluten-free soy sauce)

Per serve
Energy: 872 kj (209 cal)
Carbohydrate: 4.4g
Protein: 12.8g
Fat: 15.7g
Saturated fat: 4.2g

Cured Salmon *and* Avocado Tartare

This makes a great starter or nibble if served on crackers. Cured salmon (see page 88) is diced finely and mixed and flavoured with the other ingredients.

1 Combine mayonnaise, lime juice and wasabi paste.

2 Just before serving, mix with the diced salmon, avocado, red onion or shallots, capers and basil. Season mixture with salt and pepper to taste. Divide salmon tartare between 6 small custard cups, tea cups or ramekins. Press tartare down firmly with the back of a spoon to ensure a firm shape when tartare is unmoulded.

3 To unmould and serve, place a small serving plate on top of each mould and invert. The tartare should unmould onto the plate quite easily. Serve with a wedge of lime and lavash crackers.

SERVES: 4

PREP TIME: 15 MINUTES

Japanese mayonnaise 2 tablespoons
lime juice of 1
wasabi paste ½–1 teaspoon to taste
cured salmon gravlax (see page 88) 400–500g, cut into small dice (about ½–1cm)
avocado 1 firm ripe, diced
red onion or **shallots** 2 tablespoons finely diced
capers 2 tablespoons, finely chopped
basil leaves ¼ cup finely chopped
salt
black pepper freshly ground
lime 1, cut into wedges to serve
lavash crackers to serve

DAIRY FREE GLUTEN FREE

Per serve
Energy: 1553kj (366 cal)
Carbohydrate: 1.2g
Protein: 24.3g
Fat: 29.8g
Saturated fat: 7.1g

Thai Marinated Fish Carpaccio

You must use very fresh fish for carpaccio, as essentially you are eating raw fish. Try to cut the slices as thin as you can. The fish is briefly marinated in lime juice, then served with crisp raw vegetables, mango or papaya, kaffir lime and a bit of coconut cream.

1 Use a very sharp knife to remove any blood lines from the fish, then thinly slice flesh on an angle. Arrange slices in a flat dish. Mix lime juice, kaffir lime leaf and fish or soy sauce together and pour over fish. Set aside in fridge to marinate for 15 minutes.

2 Pour marinade off fish and reserve. Mix marinade with coconut cream and adjust seasoning with more fish or soy sauce to taste.

3 Toss papaya or mango, chilli, spring onion, coriander, crispy fried shallots and peanuts together.

4 To serve, arrange slices of marinated fish on serving plates. Top with salad and spoon over some coconut cream dressing. Serve immediately.

SERVES: 4

PREP TIME: 20 MINUTES

MARINATING TIME: 15 MINUTES

white fish very fresh, firm (e.g. kingfish, blue moki, snapper, trevally) 400g
lime juice fresh ¼ cup
kaffir lime leaf 1, central stem removed, very finely chopped
fish sauce or **soy sauce** 1½ teaspoons
coconut cream 2 tablespoons
green papaya or **mango** ½ unripe, peeled into ribbons with a vegetable peeler
red chilli 1 large, sliced
spring onions 3, shredded or thinly sliced
coriander ½ cup roughly chopped
crispy fried shallots 1½ tablespoons
roasted peanuts ¼ cup roughly chopped

DAIRY FREE   GLUTEN FREE

(Use gluten-free soy sauce)

Per serve
Energy: 844kj (202 cal)
Carbohydrate: 4.9g
Protein: 24.3g
Fat: 7.4g
Saturated fat: 2.1g

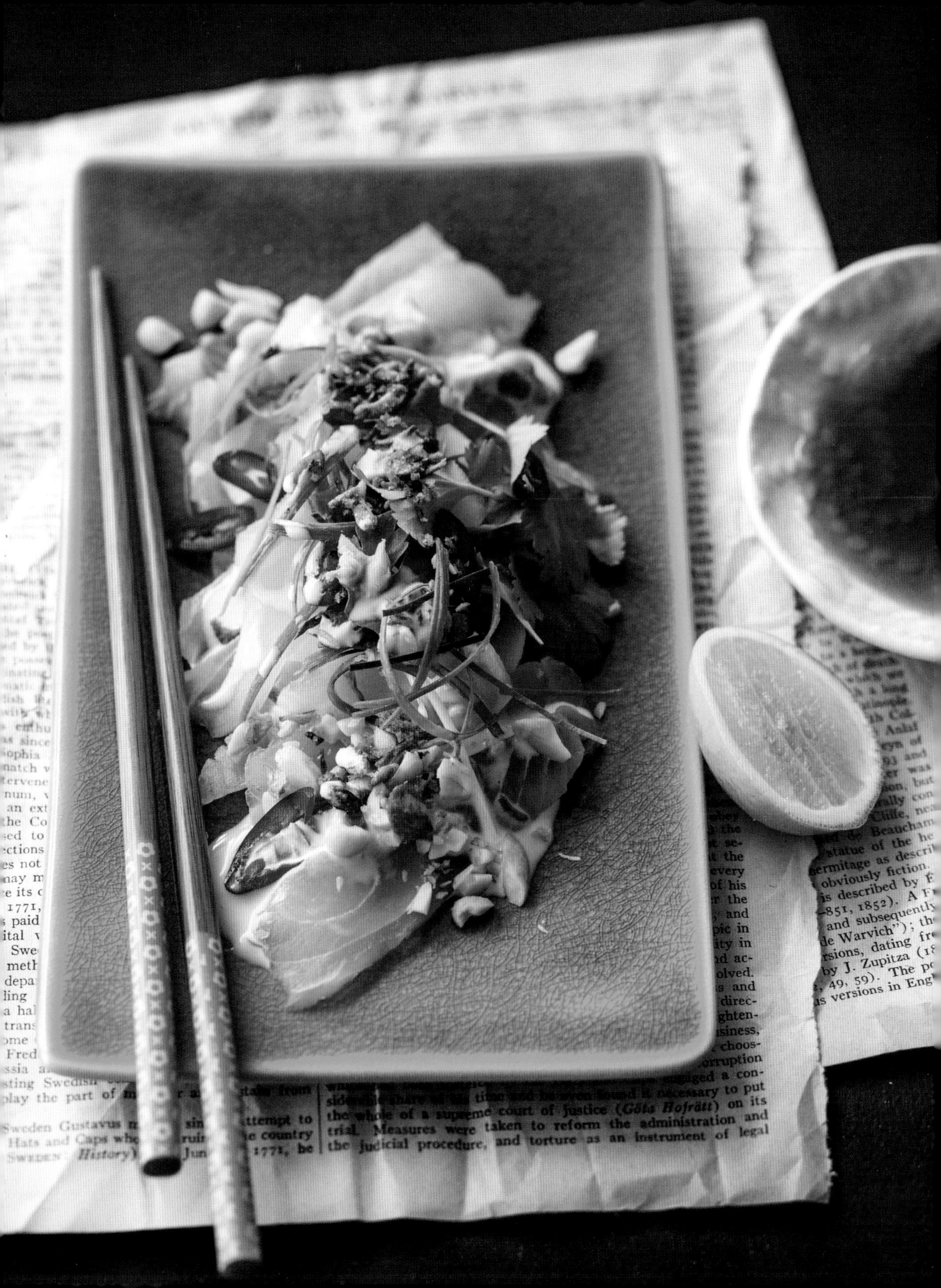

Beef Tataki *with* Apple *and* Radish

This is my take on beef tataki, a popular Japanese dish of rare beef. I serve the paper-thin slices of rare eye fillet with a sharp and tangy ponzu sauce, which is a mixture of soy sauce and lime juice. This is a delicious entrée, sure to impress.

1   Heat olive oil in a frypan on high heat. Season eye fillet with salt and pepper and sear for 30–45 seconds on all sides, so the middle is still rare. Remove and set aside to rest (and cool) for 10–15 minutes.

2   Lay a piece of cling film, about an arm's length, out on the bench and firmly wrap eye fillet up in a nice cylindrical shape, twisting the ends of the cling film to secure. Freeze wrapped eye fillet for at least 3 hours, or overnight, until firm.

3   Remove cling film from eye fillet and slice as thinly as you can with a very sharp knife. If it has frozen very hard, allow it to thaw for 20 minutes on the bench so it is easier to slice. Lay slices of beef around serving plates as you go, slightly overlapping.

4   To make the dressing, combine the ponzu dressing, shallot, chilli if using and coriander.

5   To assemble, lay radish slices in centre of plates with beef, slightly overlapping. Place a small pile of watercress, carrot and apple in the middle. Season beef with a little salt and spoon over a couple of tablespoons of dressing. Serve immediately — the beef will be at the perfect temperature, cold but not frozen.

SERVES: 4

PREP TIME: 15 MINUTES

FREEZING TIME: 3 HOURS

COOK TIME: 2–3 MINUTES

olive oil 1 tablespoon
beef eye fillet 400g (try to get a piece that is an even size along the length)
salt
black pepper freshly ground

DRESSING

ponzu dressing ¾ cup (see page 252)
shallot 1, finely chopped
red chilli 1, finely chopped (optional)
coriander 2 tablespoons chopped

TO ASSEMBLE

baby radishes 4, thinly sliced
watercress handful
carrot 1 small, shredded or peeled into ribbons with a vegetable peeler
green apple ½ (skin on), thinly sliced and cut into matchsticks

(Use gluten-free soy sauce)

Per serve
Energy: 1194kj (285 cal)
Carbohydrate: 7.4g
Protein: 24.7g
Fat: 17.7g
Saturated fat: 5.3g

Smoked Salmon, Asparagus *and* Avocado Filo Baskets

You can fill these filo baskets up with any kind of salad: salmon, asparagus and avocado is just one idea. Serve the filo baskets as soon as you fill them to ensure the pastry stays nice and crispy when you eat them.

SERVES: 4

PREP TIME: 10 MINUTES

COOK TIME: 8–10 MINUTES

filo pastry 4 sheets
butter 30g, melted
asparagus spears 1 bunch, trimmed
 and cut into 4–5cm lengths
baby rocket or other **salad greens**
 2 handfuls
avocado 1 firm ripe, chopped
cold-smoked salmon 8–12 slivers

CREAMY HERB DRESSING

crème fraîche 4 tablespoons
lemon juice of ½
flat-leaf parsley ¼ cup, finely chopped

Per serve
Energy: 1217kj (291 cal)
Carbohydrate: 12.7g
Protein: 14.3g
Fat: 25.8g
Saturated fat: 9.5g

1 Preheat oven to 180°C. Bring a saucepan of salted water to the boil. Lay a sheet of filo pastry on the bench and brush with melted butter. Repeat with remaining filo sheets, layering with melted butter in between sheets. Cut into four rectangles. Push filo rectangles into medium-sized ramekins or large muffin pans to form a basket shape. Bake in oven for 8–10 minutes or until crisp and golden.

2 Place some ice and cold water in a bowl ready to blanch asparagus. Cook asparagus in boiling water for 1–2 minutes until bright green and just tender, then drain and plunge into iced water (this ensures the asparagus will retain its colour and texture).

3 To assemble, place a filo basket on each plate. Divide rocket or salad leaves, avocado and asparagus between baskets. Arrange slices of smoked salmon on top.

4 Mix all dressing ingredients together and drizzle over top of baskets just before serving.

Lemongrass *and* Chilli Chicken Lettuce Cups

This is one of my favourite ways to start a meal. These lettuce cups, filled with a tasty mixture of chicken, lemongrass, chilli and hoisin sauce, make a great appetiser and are fun to eat. Place a pile of lettuce cups with a bowl of the filling on a platter for everyone to help themselves. Finely chopping chicken thigh meat as opposed to using minced chicken gives a much juicier, tastier result.

1 Heat oil in a wok or large frypan on high heat. Fry lemongrass, garlic, ginger and chicken for 5–6 minutes until chicken is cooked through and most of the liquid has been absorbed from the pan. Add hoisin sauce and continue cooking for 2–3 minutes. Season with salt and pepper to taste.

2 Add green beans, spring onion and chilli to chicken mixture and briefly toss before turning off heat.

3 Cut iceberg lettuce in half and gently tease leaves apart so you have lettuce 'cups'.

4 To serve, arrange lettuce cups on a large serving platter and fill with a spoonful of chicken mixture. Roll up lettuce cups and eat.

SERVES: 6

PREP TIME: 15 MINUTES

COOK TIME: 10 MINUTES

peanut or other **oil** (e.g. canola, soy or rice bran) 2 tablespoons
lemongrass 2 stalks, finely chopped
garlic 2 cloves, finely chopped
ginger 2 teaspoons grated or minced
chicken thighs 450–500g boneless, skinless, finely diced
hoisin sauce 2 heaped tablespoons
salt
pepper
green beans ½ cup thinly sliced
spring onions 4, thinly sliced
red chillies 2, finely chopped
iceberg lettuce 1

DAIRY FREE

Per serve
Energy: 683 kj (163 cal)
Carbohydrate: 5.0g
Protein: 16.8g
Fat: 8.5g
Saturated fat: 1.6g

Lime *and* Basil Cured Salmon Gravlax

Curing salmon with a mix of salt and sugar draws out moisture from the flesh, intensifying the salmon's flavour and colour, and firming up its texture. This is essentially salmon gravlax, which is traditionally flavoured with dill; however, I've used lime and basil which gives a wonderful flavour.

SERVES: 16

PREP TIME: 10 MINUTES

CURING TIME: 24–36 HOURS

fresh salmon 1 whole side or fillet (skin on), pin-boned
salt 2 tablespoons
sugar 2 tablespoons
basil leaves ½ cup, sliced
limes finely grated zest of 2

Per serve
Energy: 135.5kj (32.4 cal)
Carbohydrate: 1.6g
Protein: 1.7g
Fat: 2.2g
Saturated fat: 0.6g

1 Cut salmon fillet in half widthways. Lay the square/rectangular half on a dish or plate, skin side down. Mix salt, sugar, basil and lime zest together and sprinkle over the flesh of the salmon. Place the other (tail end) piece of salmon on top, so that the two pieces sandwich the curing mixture and the skin is facing out. Wrap securely with cling film, place another plate on top and weigh down with something heavy, e.g. a cast-iron pan or mortar and pestle. Place in the fridge for 24–36 hours.

2 Remove cling film and pour off the liquid that has seeped out of the salmon during the curing process. Wipe salmon fillets clean with a paper towel to get rid of the wilted basil and any excess salt and sugar. The salmon will be a deeper colour and the flesh much firmer (a result of extracting moisture).

3 Remove skin from salmon using a sharp knife. The salmon is now ready to be used. Slice very thinly to serve with crackers and cream cheese or crème fraîche, or make a salmon tartare (see page 79). Cured salmon will keep in the fridge for up to a week.

Barbecue Prawns *with* Spicy Mango *and* Chilli Dipping Sauce

This spicy mango dipping sauce also makes a fantastic accompaniment to barbecued chicken skewers. Or mixed with yoghurt it makes a great creamy dressing for a tossed salad with chicken or prawns, tomatoes, red onion and cos lettuce.

SERVES: 4–6

PREP TIME: 10 MINUTES

COOK TIME: 30–35 MINUTES

SPICY MANGO AND CHILLI SAUCE

capsicums 2 red
red chillies 2 large
mango 1 large ripe, peeled and roughly chopped
sweet chilli sauce 2 tablespoons
smoked paprika ¼ teaspoon
olive oil
salt
limes juice of 2

BARBECUE PRAWNS

raw prawns 2 dozen large (shell on), defrosted
coriander 2 tablespoons chopped to garnish (optional)

DAIRY FREE   GLUTEN FREE

Per serve
Energy: 480kj (115 cal)
Carbohydrate: 10.6g
Protein: 16.5g
Fat: 0.7g
Saturated fat: 0.1g

1   Preheat oven to 220°C. Place whole capsicums on an oven tray and roast for 25 minutes until skins are blackened, charred and blistered. In the last 15 minutes of cooking time, add whole chillies to roast until skin is charred.

2   Remove capsicums and chilli and leave to cool before peeling off skins (they should come off easily). Discard capsicum seeds and roughly chop flesh. Chop chilli flesh, keeping seeds. In a food processor or with a stick blender, purée capsicum, chilli, mango, sweet chilli sauce and smoked paprika.

3   Heat a drizzle of olive oil in a frypan on medium heat. Pour in sauce and simmer for 8–10 minutes until thick. Season with salt to taste and stir in lime juice. The sauce will keep in the fridge for up to a week.

4   When ready to cook prawns, preheat your barbecue to medium to high heat. Cook prawns (in their shells) for 2 minutes on each side until shell colour changes to an orange-red.

5   Reheat sauce. Serve a bowl of the sauce on a platter with prawns. Garnish with coriander if desired. To eat, peel a prawn and dip into sauce.

Kokoda

Kokoda (pronounced ko-kon-da) is one of my favourite dishes. It originates in the Pacific Islands where fresh fish is in abundance. You need really fresh fish for this recipe because essentially it is raw fish cooked from the acidity of the lime juice. It's an incredibly refreshing dish.

1 Dice fish into 1cm cubes. Combine with lime juice in a non-metal non-corrosive bowl.

2 Cover and set aside to marinate for 1 hour in the fridge — the acid of the lime juice will 'cook' the fish.

3 Mix in coconut cream, onion, chilli if using, spring onion, capsicum and tomatoes. Season to taste with salt and pepper. Serve in small bowls or in lettuce leaf cups.

SERVES: 4

PREP TIME: 5–10 MINUTES

MARINATING TIME: 1 HOUR

white fish very fresh (e.g. snapper, trevally, bluenose, terakihi) 500g boneless, skinless
lime juice fresh ²/₃ cup
coconut cream ¼ cup
red onion ½, finely diced
red chilli 1, finely chopped (optional)
spring onions 2, finely sliced
green capsicum 1 small, diced
tomatoes 2, seeds removed, diced
salt
pepper

Per serve
Energy: 672kj (161 cal)
Carbohydrate: 7.4g
Protein: 21.3g
Fat: 5.6g
Saturated fat: 2.6g

Smoky Crayfish *and* Potato Salad

If you are lucky enough to have caught some crayfish, then try out this delicious simple salad with a creamy and smoky mayonnaise dressing.

SERVES: 4

PREP TIME: 10–15 MINUTES

waxy baby potatoes 600g
Japanese mayonnaise ½ cup
chipotle sauce* 2–3 tablespoons to taste
lemon or **lime juice** 2–3 tablespoons
  to taste
cos lettuce ½ large, chopped
cherry tomatoes 1 punnet, cut in half
cooked crayfish** shredded meat of 2
coriander or **flat-leaf parsley**
  ¼ cup chopped

Per serve
Energy: 1730kj (413 cal)
Carbohydrate: 27.7g
Protein: 15.1g
Fat: 26.2g
Saturated fat: 4.7g

1 Bring a medium-sized pot of salted water to the boil. Cook potatoes in boiling salted water until just tender, 10–15 minutes. Drain and set aside to cool. When cooled, halve potatoes.

2 Mix mayonnaise with chipotle sauce and lemon or lime juice.

3 Toss chipotle mayonnaise with potatoes, cos lettuce, cherry tomatoes and crayfish meat. Divide between plates and garnish with coriander or flat-leaf parsley.

*Tip If you don't have chipotle sauce, use ¼ teaspoon smoked paprika and a pinch of cayenne pepper instead.

**Tip To humanely dispatch and cook a crayfish, put in the freezer for at least 30 minutes (it will go to sleep), then plunge a sharp knife through its head, between the eyes, before cooking in boiling salted water for 5–6 minutes.

Confetti Couscous

So called because it looks a bit like confetti. This is a great side for any meat, fish or chicken dish. If roasting a chicken, place the kumara in with the chicken for the last 30 minutes and use some of the roasting juices to toss with the couscous.

SERVES: 4–6 AS A SIDE DISH

PREP TIME: 10 MINUTES

COOK TIME: 25–30 MINUTES

orange kumara 600g (skin on), cut into 2.5cm chunks
olive oil 1 tablespoon
runny honey or **maple syrup** 1 tablespoon
salt
black pepper freshly ground
dried couscous ½ cup
boiling water ½ cup
butter or **olive oil** 1 tablespoon
orange finely grated zest of 1
shelled pistachios ¾ cup, chopped
pine nuts 1 x 70g packet, toasted
dried cranberries or **cherries** ¾ cup, chopped
parsley ½ cup finely chopped
mint leaves 1 cup, torn

(Dairy free with olive oil)

Per serve
Energy: 2091kj (499 cal)
Carbohydrate: 61.0g
Protein: 11.5g
Fat: 23.6g
Saturated fat: 4.7g

1 Preheat oven to 200°C. Line an oven tray with baking paper. Lay kumara chunks on prepared oven tray, toss with olive oil and honey or maple syrup, and season with salt and pepper. Roast for 25–30 minutes until kumara is soft and slightly caramelised.

2 In a bowl, combine couscous, boiling water, butter and a pinch of salt. Cover and leave to stand for 5–10 minutes. Fluff up grains with a fork

3 Toss couscous with orange zest, pistachios, pinenuts, cranberries or cherries, parsley, mint and roast kumara.

Roast Yams *and* Carrots *with* Honey, Coriander *and* Dukkah

This is a great side dish with any roast meat, but also good enough to eat on its own! Drizzling a bit of honey on the vegetables before roasting helps them caramelise. You could also use parsnips and Jerusalem artichokes in place of the carrots and yams.

SERVES: 4–6 AS A SIDE DISH

PREP TIME: 5–10 MINUTES

COOK TIME: 25–30 MINUTES

carrots 3, peeled and cut into batons
red yams 16–20 small, cut in half lengthways
olive oil 1–2 tablespoons
runny honey 2 tablespoons
dukkah 2 tablespoons
salt
black pepper freshly ground
sesame oil ½ teaspoon
coriander ½ cup chopped

DAIRY FREE | GLUTEN FREE | VEG

Per serve
Energy: 174kj (41 cal)
Carbohydrate: 31.1g
Protein: 2.0g
Fat: 5.6g
Saturated fat: 1.2g

1 Preheat oven to 200°C. Line an oven tray with baking paper. Place carrots and yams on prepared tray and drizzle over olive oil and honey, tossing to coat. Sprinkle over dukkah and season with salt and pepper. Roast for 25–30 minutes until vegetables are soft and slightly caramelised.

2 Drizzle over sesame oil and toss with coriander just before serving.

Dill, Caper *and* Asparagus Potatoes

This is a yummy summer side dish using baby new potatoes and asparagus. It goes well with fish, chicken and meat. Green beans make a good alternative if asparagus is not available.

SERVES: 6 AS A SIDE DISH

PREP TIME: 5 MINUTES

COOK TIME: 12–15 MINUTES

waxy baby potatoes 800g
asparagus 1 bunch, trimmed and halved
capers 1½–2 tablespoons, chopped
dill paste 1 tablespoon, or **fresh dill**
  ¼ cup, chopped
Dijon mustard 1 tablespoon
butter softened or **extra virgin olive oil**
  2 tablespoons
salt
black pepper freshly ground

DAIRY FREE   GLUTEN FREE

(Dairy free with olive oil)

Per serve
Energy: 631kj (151 cal)
Carbohydrate: 23.0g
Protein: 4.0g
Fat: 4.8g
Saturated fat: 2.9g

1   Bring a large saucepan of salted water to the boil. Cut any larger potatoes in half so they are all roughly the same size. Cook potatoes in boiling salted water until just tender (when the tip of a sharp knife goes through easily), 10–12 minutes. Add asparagus to the potatoes and cook for 2 minutes more.

2   Drain asparagus and potatoes and toss with capers, dill paste or dill, Dijon mustard and butter. Season to taste with salt and pepper and serve warm.

dinners

The power of the dinner table can't be under-estimated. Dinner time is significant for healthy living, in more ways than just what you eat. Aside from being the main meal that families and couples can share together regularly, it is also the time when healthy eating practices are most likely to be learned and developed.

Those who eat at a table with others are much less likely to over-eat, a result of slower and more mindful eating, without the distractions of modern-day technology. Aim to enjoy dinner over at least 15–20 minutes, as it takes this long for the hunger hormone leptin to signal to your brain that you are full — fast eaters end up eating more. Eat until you are no longer hungry, but not until you are full, and remember to follow the plate model — one-quarter carbs, one-quarter protein and half vegetables.

Children who eat at a table with others are also more likely to try new foods and eat a wider variety (including vegetables). Getting your kids involved in food preparation from a young age has huge benefits to their health — learning how to cook means they won't rely on processed foods and takeaways when they leave home.

Throughout the week, it's good practice to aim for at least two meat-free meals, one or two fish meals, and the rest meat or poultry. So this chapter is organised into vegetarian, fish, poultry and meat meals. Many can be prepared in 30 minutes or less so you can enjoy healthy 'fast food' throughout the week, while others are suitable for freezing in portions for those busy nights — all you have to do is reheat and serve, avoiding falling into the takeaways trap.

I trust some of these recipes will become family favourites, and bring you together at dinner time to create lasting memories of good food and laughter around the table.

Broccoli, Kale, Mushroom, Tofu *and* Peanut Noodles

The key to a good stir-fry is having all the ingredients chopped and prepared before you begin cooking, as once you start the process is very quick. A high heat and not over-crowding the wok are also key, which is why ingredients are stir-fried in batches. Use a firm tofu for this recipe. If you don't like tofu, substitute with thin strips of chicken or beef.

1 Bring a medium-sized saucepan of water to the boil. Heat 1 tablespoon of the oil in a wok or large frypan on high heat. Wash broccoli or broccolini and kale or leafy greens and shake off excess water. Add ginger, garlic and slightly damp greens to hot wok (a few water droplets on the vegetables will help create steam to cook them evenly). Stir-fry for 2–3 minutes until vegetables are bright green and tender. Remove from wok and set aside.

2 Heat another tablespoon of oil in the same frypan and add mushrooms. Stir-fry for 2–3 minutes until cooked through. Remove from pan and set aside with the greens.

3 Heat remaining tablespoon of oil in the same pan and add tofu cubes. Stir-fry for 2–3 minutes until light golden brown. Return broccoli, kale and mushrooms to the pan and toss for 1–2 minutes to warm through.

4 Cook soba noodles in boiling water until just cooked (do not overcook), about 4 minutes. Drain and toss with soy and hoisin dressing, cooked greens, mushrooms, tofu and peanuts. Garnish with chilli and coriander if using.

SERVES: 2–3

PREP TIME: 10 MINUTES

COOK TIME: 10–15 MINUTES

peanut or other **oil** (e.g. canola, soy or rice bran) 3 tablespoons
broccoli ½ head, chopped into florets or **broccolini** 1 small bunch (about 6 stems), trimmed and halved
kale leaves or other **green leafy vegetables** (e.g. spinach or silverbeet) 2–3 large handfuls, tough stems removed, chopped
ginger 2.5cm piece, peeled, sliced and cut into thin matchsticks
garlic 2 cloves, sliced
mushrooms (e.g. portobello or button) 2 cups sliced
firm tofu 150g, cut into 2cm cubes
dried soba noodles 160–180g
soy and hoisin dressing ¼ cup (see page 252)
roasted peanuts ½ cup, roughly chopped
chilli 1 chopped to garnish (optional)
coriander 2 tablespoons chopped to garnish (optional)

DAIRY FREE · VEG

Per serve
Energy: 2142kj (512 cal)
Carbohydrate: 43.0g
Protein: 23.3g
Fat: 31.1g
Saturated fat: 4.6g

Chickpea, Tomato, Spinach *and* Paneer Curry

This is one hell of a tasty vegetarian curry; it'll even please diehard carnivores. Paneer is an Indian cheese similar to haloumi, which holds its shape when cooked. It adds a subtle creamy flavour but is low in fat compared to other cheeses. Use haloumi if you can't find paneer.

SERVES: 4–5

PREP TIME: 15 MINUTES

COOK TIME: 20–25 MINUTES

oil (e.g. canola, soy or rice bran) 3 tablespoons
onions 2 large, sliced
garlic 2 cloves, minced
ground cumin 1 teaspoon
ground coriander 1 teaspoon
turmeric powder ½ teaspoon
chilli powder ½ teaspoon (optional)
green capsicum 1, sliced
ginger 2cm piece, peeled, thinly sliced and cut into matchsticks
tomato paste 2 tablespoons
sugar 2 teaspoons
crushed tomatoes 1 x 400g can
vegetable or **chicken stock** 1 cup
chickpeas 1 x 400g can, drained
paneer cheese 300g, cut into 2cm cubes
baby spinach 2–3 large handfuls
salt
black pepper freshly ground
lemon juice of ½

TO SERVE

natural unsweetened Greek yoghurt ⅓ cup
coriander ¾ cup, chopped
plain steamed rice (see page 251)
cucumber, sliced
carrot, shredded

1 Heat oil in a large frypan, wok or saucepan on medium heat. Cook onion and garlic until onion is golden brown, 8–10 minutes.

2 Add spices, capsicum and ginger and continue cooking, stirring constantly, for a further 2 minutes until capsicum has softened. Add tomato paste, sugar, crushed tomatoes, vegetable or chicken stock and chickpeas. Bring to the boil, then reduce heat to a simmer and add paneer. Continue simmering for 10–15 minutes until the curry has thickened slightly and the paneer is soft.

3 Add spinach to hot curry and stir through until wilted. Season to taste with salt, pepper and lemon juice.

4 Serve curry, garnished with Greek yoghurt and coriander, rice and a salad of sliced cucumber and shredded carrot in large bowls in the middle of the table for everyone to help themselves.

GLUTEN FREE   VEG

Per serve
Energy: 2423kj (579 cal)
Carbohydrate: 67.3g
Protein: 25.3g
Fat: 22.1g
Saturated fat: 7.6g

Protein

Veges

Carbs

Curry Crushed Potatoes *with* Haloumi *and* Poached Egg

This is one of my favourite vegetarian meals. I love haloumi: best straight from the pan when it is still warm and golden on the outside and melted on the inside — yum!

SERVES: 4

PREP TIME: 10 MINUTES

COOK TIME: 20 MINUTES

CURRY CRUSHED POTATOES

Agria potatoes 4 medium (about 800g), scrubbed and cut into 2.5cm cubes
olive oil 3 tablespoons
onion 1, chopped
curry powder 2 teaspoons
spinach leaves 2–3 cups chopped, or **baby spinach**
lemon juice of 1
salt
black pepper freshly ground
oil (e.g. canola, soy or rice bran) for cooking

HALOUMI AND POACHED EGG

haloumi cheese 150–200g, cut into 1cm-thick slices
eggs 4

TO SERVE

mayonnaise 3 tablespoons
natural unsweetened Greek yoghurt 3 tablespoons
coriander or **flat-leaf parsley** ½ cup chopped

1 Bring a medium-sized pot of salted water to the boil. Cook potatoes in boiling salted water until just cooked through, about 8–10 minutes. Drain well.

2 Heat half of the olive oil in a large frypan on medium heat and cook onion until soft, 3–4 minutes. Add remaining olive oil, curry powder and cooked potatoes, toss and cook until potatoes start to fall apart or become a bit 'crushed', 5–6 minutes. Add spinach and lemon juice and toss with potatoes until spinach has wilted, 1–2 minutes. Season with salt and pepper to taste.

3 Heat a drizzle of oil in a frypan (preferably non-stick) on medium heat and fry haloumi slices for 1–2 minutes on each side until golden brown.

4 Bring a medium-sized saucepan of water to a gentle boil, reduce to a simmer, and carefully crack in eggs. Poach for 2 minutes until whites are just set, but yolk is still runny.

5 Mix mayonnaise with yoghurt. To serve, divide potato mixture between plates, top with a poached egg and 2 slices of haloumi. Garnish with coriander or flat-leaf parsley and serve with a dollop of yoghurt mayonnaise to the side.

GLUTEN FREE   VEG

Per serve
Energy: 2120kj (506 cal)
Carbohydrate: 41.3g
Protein: 19.5g
Fat: 30.1g
Saturated fat: 12.3g

Caramelised Baby Leek *and* Butternut Filo Pie

Using filo pastry makes a lighter pie with a frilly, crispy edge. Make sure the leeks and butternut are nicely caramelised before adding them to the pie — this will greatly improve the flavour.

1 Preheat oven to 200°C. Line an oven tray with baking paper. Cut larger baby leeks in half lengthways. Lay butternut cubes and baby leeks on prepared oven tray. Drizzle with olive oil and honey and toss to coat. Season with salt and roast for 20–25 minutes until vegetables are soft and slightly caramelised.

2 Meanwhile, whisk eggs, crème fraîche, milk, cheese and thyme together. Set aside.

3 Brush a pie dish with butter or oil. Lay 2 sheets of filo pastry in pie dish, brush lightly with butter or oil, rotate dish slightly less than 90 degrees and repeat with 2 more filo sheets and butter or oil, then rotate dish again and repeat with remaining 2 filo sheets and butter or oil. The filo should be overhanging the dish evenly on all sides. Leave excess overhanging sides.

4 Scatter caramelised butternut and sundried tomatoes evenly over pie base. Arrange baby leeks on top. Pour over egg mixture evenly. Gather up overhanging filo and crinkle up to form a frilly edge around the pie. Bake for 20 minutes until just set. Remove from oven and allow pie to rest for 10 minutes after cooking. To serve, cut pie into pieces and serve with a simple tomato and lettuce salad on the side.

SERVES: 6

PREP TIME: 15 MINUTES

COOK TIME: 40 MINUTES

butternut 400–500g (skin off), cut into 1–2cm cubes
baby leeks 200g (about 10), trimmed and washed
olive oil 1 tablespoon
honey 2 teaspoons
salt
eggs 4
crème fraîche 150g
milk ¼ cup
cheese (e.g. gouda, gruyère, Swiss, cheddar) ¾ cup grated
thyme leaves 1½ tablespoons chopped
olive oil or **melted butter** 3 tablespoons
filo pastry 6 sheets
sundried tomatoes ¼ cup chopped

VEG

Per serve
Energy: 1551kj (370 cal)
Carbohydrate: 42.7g
Protein: 12.9g
Fat: 28.6g
Saturated fat: 10.8g

Roast Stuffed Eggplant
with Greek Salad

There are many variations on stuffed eggplant recipes from the Mediterranean, where this vegetable is so plentiful. Try stuffing them with whatever takes your fancy — feta cheese, herbs, cooked potato cubes, couscous . . . the list is endless.

1 Preheat oven to 200°C. Cut eggplants in half lengthways, leaving stems intact. Place cut side up on a baking tray. Drizzle with olive oil and season with salt. Bake for 30 minutes until soft and lightly browned.

2 While eggplant is baking, make the tomato sauce. Heat olive oil in a frypan on medium heat and cook onion and garlic until soft, 3–4 minutes. Add cumin, tomato paste, crushed tomatoes and sugar. Simmer, stirring frequently, until thick and the consistency of chutney, 8–10 minutes. Season to taste with salt and pepper.

3 When eggplants have finished baking, remove from oven and scoop out the soft flesh with a spoon, being careful not to tear the skin. Mix soft eggplant flesh into tomato sauce. Lightly mix tomato eggplant sauce with cooked rice and parmesan. Fill eggplant halves with mixture, dividing equally. Drizzle over olive oil and sprinkle with pine nuts and more parmesan. Return to oven for 10 minutes until parmesan has melted.

4 To make the Greek salad, combine all ingredients and dress with lemon juice and olive oil just before serving. Serve 1 eggplant half per person, with Greek salad on the side.

SERVES: 4

PREP TIME: 15 MINUTES

COOK TIME: 40 MINUTES

ROAST STUFFED EGGPLANT

purple eggplant 2
olive oil 1 tablespoon + extra for drizzling
salt
onion 1, chopped
garlic 1 clove, finely chopped
ground cumin ½ teaspoon
tomato paste 2 tablespoons
crushed tomatoes ½ x 400g can
sugar 1 teaspoon
black pepper freshly ground
cooked brown or **wild rice** 1½ cups
(see page 251)
parmesan cheese ¼ cup grated + extra
for sprinkling
pine nuts 2–3 tablespoons

GREEK SALAD

tomatoes 3–4, chopped
telegraph cucumber 1, diced
red onion ½ small, thinly sliced
kalamata olives ½ cup chopped
feta 50g, crumbled
mint leaves ¼ cup sliced
lemon juice of 1 to dress
extra virgin olive oil to dress

Per serve
Energy: 1305kj (312 cal)
Carbohydrate: 39.6g
Protein: 12.3g
Fat: 11.9g
Saturated fat: 3.3g

Eggplant, Portobello Mushroom *and* Mozzarella Free-form Lasagne

This recipe uses an 'assemble' approach to create a tasty vegetable lasagne in a third of the time it would normally take to make. Good-quality pesto, buffalo mozzarella and fresh lasagne sheets are key.

SERVES: 2

PREP TIME: 10 MINUTES

COOK TIME: 20 MINUTES

olive oil 2 tablespoons
thyme leaves 1½ teaspoons finely chopped
garlic 1 clove, minced
portobello mushrooms 4 large, stalks removed
eggplant 4 x 1–1.5cm-thick slices
salt

TO ASSEMBLE AND SERVE

fresh lasagne 1 large sheet, cut into 6 x 10–12cm squares
tomato sauce ⅓ cup (see page 120)
basil pesto 3 tablespoons
buffalo mozzarella 1 large ball, cut into 4 slices
basil leaves to garnish

VEG

Per serve
Energy: 1692kj (404 cal)
Carbohydrate: 12.4g
Protein: 17.6g
Fat: 30.8g
Saturated fat: 8.3g

1 Preheat oven to 180°C. Line an oven tray with baking paper. Mix olive oil, thyme and garlic together. Place mushrooms (gill side up) and eggplant slices on prepared tray and spoon or brush over flavoured oil, dividing equally. Season with salt and bake for 20 minutes until eggplant is lightly browned.

2 Bring a large saucepan or frypan of salted water to the boil and cook lasagne squares until al dente, about 4 minutes. Drain and set aside.

3 Heat tomato sauce and pesto briefly in microwave.

4 To assemble, place a square of lasagne on each plate, top with a portobello mushroom and a slice of eggplant, a heaped tablespoon of tomato sauce, a heaped teaspoon of basil pesto and a slice of mozzarella. Repeat once more so you have two full layers. Top with a final square of lasagne and spoonful of tomato sauce and basil pesto. Garnish with basil leaves before serving.

Porcini Mushroom, Sage *and* Spinach Risotto

Using dried mushrooms, as well as fresh, is the secret to this risotto's intense mushroom flavour. The perfect risotto should be saucy in texture, just wet enough to spread like lava if you tilt the plate, not clumpy and stodgy. Other dried mushrooms also work well in this recipe (e.g. chaterelles, shiitake, oyster).

SERVES: 2–3

PREP TIME: 15 MINUTES

COOK TIME: 35 MINUTES

dried sliced porcini mushrooms 30g
boiling water 2 cups
vegetable or **chicken stock** 1½ cups
butter 25g
onion 1, finely chopped
garlic 2 cloves, finely chopped
Arborio or **Carnaroli rice** 1 cup
dry white wine 1 cup
parmesan cheese ¾ cup grated + extra to serve (optional)
salt
black pepper freshly ground
butter 25g
sage leaves 2–3 tablespoons sliced
button mushrooms 100g, quartered
spinach leaves 2 handfuls, chopped

GLUTEN FREE   VEG

Per serve
Energy: 1565kj (374 cal)
Carbohydrate: 5.1g
Protein: 14.7g
Fat: 25.0g
Saturated fat: 15.1g

1 Soak dried mushrooms in boiling water for 10–15 minutes until mushrooms are soft (you will use the soaking liquid later on). Heat vegetable or chicken stock in a saucepan on the stove top.

2 Heat first measure of butter in a large frypan on medium heat and sauté onion and garlic until soft, 3–4 minutes. Add rice and cook for 2 minutes, stirring constantly, until lightly toasted. Add wine and allow to boil until it is mostly absorbed by the rice, about 2 minutes.

3 Drain soaked porcini mushrooms, reserving the soaking liquid. Mix 1½ cups of mushroom soaking liquid with the heated stock and add this to the rice. Stir, cover frypan with a lid and reduce to low heat. Leave to cook for 15–20 minutes, stirring very gently once or twice during cooking, until rice is tender but grains are still intact. There will still be a little liquid left over — as the rice cools it will absorb most of this.

4 Roughly chop porcini mushrooms and stir into risotto along with parmesan cheese. Season to taste with salt and pepper.

5 Heat second measure of butter in a frypan on medium heat. Cook sage and button mushrooms for 2 minutes. Add spinach and cook for a further 1–2 minutes until spinach has wilted.

6 To serve, spoon some risotto onto plates and top with sage, button mushrooms and spinach. Sprinkle over extra parmesan cheese if desired.

Roast Butternut, Barley *and* Lentil Peasant Salad

I called this peasant salad because lentils and barley were traditionally considered a poor person's food. They are inexpensive, yet very rich in nutrients and fibre — we could all benefit from eating more of them!

SERVES: 4

PREP TIME: 15 MINUTES

COOK TIME: 25–30 MINUTES

butternut ½ large or 1 small (skin on), halved lengthways and cut into 1cm-thick moons
carrots 3, peeled, cut into batons
honey to drizzle
olive oil to drizzle
salt
beetroot 3, cut into 2cm-thick wedges
dried Puy lentils ½ cup
pearl barley ¼ cup

DRESSING

olive oil 3 tablespoons
garlic 3 cloves, minced
shallots 2, finely chopped
ground cumin 1 heaped teaspoon
rosemary 1 tablespoon finely chopped
thyme leaves 1 tablespoon finely chopped
chilli flakes ½–1 teaspoon
lemon finely grated zest and juice of 1
sugar 1 teaspoon
chicken or **vegetable stock powder** 1 teaspoon
red wine vinegar 3 tablespoons

baby rocket or **spinach** 4 handfuls
dukkah 2 tablespoons
feta 80–100g, crumbled

(VEG)

Per serve
Energy: 1858kj (444 cal)
Carbohydrate: 53.2g
Protein: 19.2g
Fat: 15.0g
Saturated fat: 4.6g

1 Preheat oven to 190°C. Line 2 oven trays with baking paper. Place butternut and carrots on a prepared tray, drizzle with olive oil and honey and season with salt. Place beetroot on the other prepared tray, drizzle with olive oil and honey and season with salt. Roast vegetables for 25–30 minutes until slightly caramelised.

2 Place Puy lentils and barley in a saucepan with plenty of cold water. Cover, bring to the boil and cook for 15–20 minutes or until lentils and barley are just tender but still with a bit of bite. Drain and set aside.

3 To make the dressing, heat olive oil in a frypan on medium heat. Cook garlic and shallots for 2 minutes until soft. Add cumin, rosemary, thyme, chilli and lemon zest and fry for a further 2 minutes. Add lemon juice, sugar, stock powder and vinegar. Add lentils and barley and toss with the dressing.

4 Just before serving, toss mesclun salad or baby spinach leaves with lentils and roast vegetables. Divide between plates, and sprinkle with dukkah and feta.

Beetroot, Thyme *and* Goat's Cheese Tarts *with* Pear *and* Rocket Salad

Beetroot, thyme and goat's cheese really complement each other in this simple but delicious tart. I prefer to use a soft creamy goat's cheese, but you can also use cow's feta instead. Make smaller tarts to serve as an entrée.

1 Preheat oven to 200°C. Wrap each whole beetroot in tinfoil. Bake for 30–35 minutes or until soft (when a skewer goes right through without resistance). Allow beetroot to cool, then rub off skins and slice into 1cm-thick rounds.

2 Roll out pastry sheets by approximately 2.5cm on one side. Use a small plate (roughly 14cm diameter) to cut out two circles from each sheet of pastry. Alternatively, for rectangular-shaped tarts, simply cut each pastry sheet in half.

3 Place pieces of pastry on a baking tray. Arrange slices of beetroot around the edge of the pastry, slightly overlapping. Mix thyme, honey and olive oil together and brush over beetroot. Top with chunks of goat's cheese. Bake for 15–20 minutes or until pastry is puffed and golden.

4 Just before serving, toss rocket, pear slices and walnuts with balsamic vinegar and extra virgin olive oil. Serve one tart per person with salad on the side.

SERVES: 4

PREP TIME: 10–15 MINUTES + 30–35 MINUTES TO COOK BEETROOT

COOK TIME: 15–20 MINUTES

TARTS

beetroot 4 medium, topped and tailed
puff pastry 2 square sheets
thyme leaves 2 teaspoons finely chopped
runny honey 1 tablespoon
olive oil 1½ tablespoons
soft goat's cheese 100g

PEAR AND ROCKET SALAD

baby rocket 4 handfuls
pear 1 firm ripe, sliced
walnuts 2–3 tablespoons chopped
balsamic vinegar to dress
extra virgin olive oil to dress

Per serve
Energy: 1676kj (400 cal)
Carbohydrate: 39.0g
Protein: 9.9g
Fat: 22.7g
Saturated fat: 12.8g

Tomato, Broccolini,
Pine Nut *and* Parmesan
Fettucine

This tomato sauce is handy to make in bulk and freeze for a quick meal. You can use chopped broccoli in place of broccolini or, in summer, cubes of cooked eggplant are nice.

SERVES: 4

PREP TIME: 10 MINUTES

COOK TIME: 20–25 MINUTES

TOMATO SAUCE

olive oil 2 tablespoons
onions 2, chopped
garlic 3 cloves, chopped
crushed tomatoes 2 x 400g cans
tomato paste ¼ cup
sugar 1½ teaspoons
extra virgin olive oil 2 tablespoons
salt
black pepper freshly ground

PASTA

dried fettucine 360–400g
broccolini 1 bunch (8–10 stems), chopped
basil leaves large handful to serve
parmesan cheese ½–1 cup grated
    to serve
toasted pine nuts 3–4 tablespoons
    (see page 251)

(Dairy free without parmesan)

Per serve
Energy: 2161kj (516 cal)
Carbohydrate: 45.3g
Protein: 17.8g
Fat: 29.3g
Saturated fat: 6.1g

1 Bring a large saucepan of salted water to the boil. To make the tomato sauce, heat olive oil in a large frypan on medium heat and sauté onion and garlic until onion is soft, about 10 minutes. Add crushed tomatoes, tomato paste and sugar and simmer for 10–15 minutes until sauce has reduced and thickened. Stir through extra virgin olive oil, and season to taste with salt and pepper.

2 Cook fettucine in boiling salted water for 8–10 minutes until just cooked (al dente). Two minutes before fettucine is cooked, add broccolini to boiling water to cook with fettucine. Drain, reserving ¼ cup of the pasta cooking water.

3 Toss fettucine and broccolini with tomato sauce, reserved pasta water and most of the basil leaves. Divide between bowls and top with more basil, parmesan cheese and pine nuts.

Tip This tomato sauce keeps in the fridge for up to a week and freezes well, which, when prepared ahead, makes for a quick meal.

Crispy-skin Fish
with Asian Slaw

This Asian slaw is packed full of fresh flavour. The key is the perfect balance of sweet, salty, sour and hot in the dressing, the crispness of the shredded cabbage and the crunch of the roasted peanuts. So moreish, it makes eating a huge amount of vegetables extremely easy. Served with a piece of fish, it doesn't get healthier or more delicious than this!

1 Season fish with salt. Heat oil in a large frypan on medium heat and pan-fry fish, skin side down, for 2–3 minutes until skin is crispy. Flatten the fish with a fish slice so that all the skin makes contact with the pan. Flip fish over and cook for 1 minute or until fish is just cooked through.

2 Toss cabbage, mango, carrot, peanuts, crispy shallots if using, spring onion and coriander with dressing just before serving. To serve, divide Asian slaw and fish between plates.

Tip Serve with coconut rice (see page 131) to make into a more substantial meal

*Tip Shred cabbage and carrot by cutting it very finely with a sharp knife. To julienne mango, first peel the mango with a vegetable peeler, cut thin slices of mango, then cut slices into thin matchsticks.

SERVES: 4

PREP TIME: 15 MINUTES

COOK TIME: 5–10 MINUTES

CRISPY-SKIN FISH

snapper fillets 4 x 120–150g (skin on)
salt
oil (e.g. canola, soy or rice bran)
   2 tablespoons

ASIAN SLAW

cabbage* 2 cups shredded
green mango* 1, peeled and julienned
carrot* 1, peeled and shredded or grated
roasted peanuts ¾ cup, roughly
   chopped
crispy fried shallots ¼ cup (storebought,
   optional)
spring onions 3, sliced
coriander ¼ cup chopped
lime and sesame dressing ½ cup
   (see page 252)

DAIRY FREE   GLUTEN FREE

Per serve
Energy: 2019kj (482 cal)
Carbohydrate: 19.9g
Protein: 38.8g
Fat: 28.0g
Saturated fat: 4.1g

Salmon Tom Yum

This light and tasty meal is quick to put together and will warm you up in colder weather. Thin slices of raw salmon are added to the hot soup, which cook perfectly in the residual heat.

SERVES: 4

PREP TIME: 10 MINUTES

COOK TIME: 10 MINUTES

dried soba or **udon noodles** 320g
tom yum paste 4–5 tablespoons
chicken or **fish stock (unsalted)**
   good-quality fresh 1 litre
water 500ml
cherry tomatoes 1 punnet
button mushrooms 10–12, sliced
soft tofu 100g, sliced
baby bok choy 4, halved lengthways
fish or **soy sauce** to taste
salmon fillet 350–400g (skin off), fresh,
   pin-boned and sliced
mung bean sprouts large handful
coriander ½ cup chopped
mint ½ cup chopped
lime 1, cut into wedges

DAIRY FREE   GLUTEN FREE

(Use gluten-free soy sauce and buckwheat soba noodles)

Per serve
Energy: 2352kj (562 cal)
Carbohydrate: 43.7g
Protein: 41.7g
Fat: 25.1g
Saturated fat: 7.0g

1   Cook noodles according to packet instructions until just cooked through, about 4 minutes (do not overcook). Drain and divide between serving bowls.

2   Mix tom yum paste with stock and water in a large saucepan and bring to the boil. Add cherry tomatoes, mushrooms, tofu and bok choy and cook for 3–4 minutes. Season soup with fish sauce or soy sauce to taste.

3   To serve, divide hot broth and contents between bowls of noodles and add slices of fresh salmon (the heat of the soup will cook the salmon). Top each bowl with some mung bean sprouts and garnish with coriander and mint. Squeeze over lime just before eating.

Lime *and* Sweet Chilli Glazed Salmon *with* Japanese Rice *and* Greens

If you want a meal that is packed full of nutritional goodies and quick and delicious then look no further. I can't recall how many times I have fallen back on this ridiculously easy recipe on nights when I arrive home late but still want a healthy, tasty dinner. Unlike other fish, raw salmon freezes well, so can be frozen in handy portions.

SERVES: 4

PREP TIME: 10 MINUTES

COOK TIME: 20–25 MINUTES

JAPANESE RICE

brown or **white rice** 1½ cups
water 2¼ cups
soy sauce 1½–2 tablespoons
butter knob of
toasted sesame seeds 1 tablespoon (see page 251)

GLAZED SALMON

salmon fillets 4 x 120–150g (skin on), pin-boned
sweet chilli sauce 2 tablespoons
lime finely grated zest and juice of 1
ginger 2cm piece, peeled, thinly sliced and cut into thin matchsticks
salt
black pepper freshly ground

GREENS

baby bok choy 6, halved lengthways
sesame oil 1 teaspoon
soy sauce 2 teaspoons

DAIRY FREE   GLUTEN FREE

(Use gluten-free soy sauce)
(Dairy free without butter)

Per serve
Energy: 2583 kj (618 cal)
Carbohydrate: 61.3g
Protein: 24.6g
Fat: 30.9g
Saturated fat: 9.2g

1   Preheat oven grill to 220°C. Combine rice and water in a medium-sized saucepan. Stir and bring to the boil. Cover with a tight-fitting lid and reduce to lowest heat. Cook on very low heat for 15 minutes (do not lift lid during cooking). Turn off heat and leave rice to steam, covered (again, do not lift lid), for a further 8 minutes. Uncover rice, fluff up grains with a fork and mix in soy sauce, butter and sesame seeds.

2   While rice is steaming, cook the salmon. Line an oven tray with baking paper and place salmon fillets on top, skin side down.

3   Mix together sweet chilli sauce, lime zest and juice, and ginger and spoon over salmon. Season with salt and pepper. Grill for 6–7 minutes or until salmon is just cooked through.

4   Bring a large saucepan of water to the boil. Dunk bok choy into boiling water for 1–2 minutes to cook. Drain well and toss with sesame oil and soy sauce. To serve, spoon some rice onto each plate and top with a piece of salmon and three bok choy halves.

Chinese Steamed Fish Parcels *with* Coconut Rice *and* Broccolini

This would have to be one of my favourite midweek meals. The aromatic flavours in the fish and coconut rice are bang on. Here I've served it with broccolini, but you can also serve it with other green vegetables such as bok choy, gai lan or spinach.

SERVES: 4

PREP TIME: 10 MINUTES

COOK TIME: 20–25 MINUTES

COCONUT RICE

jasmine rice 1½ cups
coconut milk 1 x can 400ml
water 1⅔ cups
ginger 4 slices (optional)
kaffir lime leaves 2 (optional)
salt pinch of

FISH AND BROCCOLINI

white fish fillets (e.g. snapper, gurnard or terakihi) 4 x 150g
soy sauce 2 tablespoons
sesame oil 2 teaspoons
garlic 1 clove, minced
red chilli 1, chopped (optional)
coriander 1 small bunch (stems and leaves), roughly chopped
ginger 2cm piece, peeled, finely sliced and cut into thin matchsticks
broccolini 2 bunches (about 20 stems), trimmed

(Use gluten-free soy sauce)

Per serve
Energy: 2208kj (527 cal)
Carbohydrate: 79.6g
Protein: 35.8g
Fat: 7.5g
Saturated fat: 1.6g

1 To make the coconut rice, combine all ingredients in a medium-sized saucepan. Stir and bring to the boil. Cover with a tight-fitting lid and reduce to lowest heat. Cook on a very low heat for 15 minutes (do not lift lid during cooking). Turn off heat and leave rice, covered (again, do not lift lid), to steam for a further 8 minutes. Uncover rice, remove ginger slices and lime leaves if using, and fluff up grains with a fork.

2 While the rice is cooking, prepare fish and broccolini. Preheat oven to 180ºC. Lay large rectangles of tinfoil (about 40cm long) on the bench and place a fish fillet in the centre of each. Mix together soy sauce, sesame oil, garlic, chilli if using, chopped coriander stems (reserve the leaves for garnish) and ginger. Spoon mixture over each fish fillet, dividing equally. Fold over tinfoil and wrap up to form parcels. Place on an oven tray and bake for 6–7 minutes until the fish is just cooked through.

3 Steam or stir-fry broccolini until bright green and tender.

4 To serve, spoon some coconut rice onto each plate. Place a fish parcel and some broccolini next to rice. Peel back tinfoil to reveal the steamed fish and garnish with chopped coriander leaves.

Cajun Fish Tacos *with* Mango Salsa *and* Chipotle Sour Cream

This is a fun, easy meal the kids can make and the whole family will love. What's even better is that with a pair of helping hands you can get this meal on the table in 10 minutes. The chipotle yoghurt is delicious and much healthier than sour cream. You can use chicken instead of fish — omit the flour (just dust in Cajun spice) and cook for 1–2 minutes more until the chicken is cooked through.

1 Preheat oven to 180°C. In a bowl, mix flour, Cajun seasoning and salt. Dust pieces of fish with seasoned flour.

2 Heat oil in a large frypan (preferably non-stick) on medium heat. Cook flour-coated fish pieces in hot oil until light golden, about 1 minute on each side — you will need to cook the fish in batches to avoid overcrowding the pan. Drain cooked pieces of fish on paper towels.

3 Heat taco shells in preheated oven according to packet instructions (generally about 5 minutes in a 180°C oven).

4 Mix sour cream and Greek yoghurt with chipotle sauce to taste.

5 Mix tomatoes, mango, avocado and coriander together to make the salsa.

6 Serve tacos, fish bites, chipotle sour cream and salsa in bowls in the middle of the table for everyone to assemble their own tacos. Stuff each taco with 4–5 fish bites, a good spoon of salsa and chipotle sour cream. Accompany with lime or lemon wedges to squeeze over the fish just before eating.

SERVES: 4–5

PREP TIME: 15 MINUTES

COOK TIME: 15 MINUTES

FISH TACOS

plain flour 2 tablespoons
Cajun seasoning 3 heaped teaspoons
salt 1 teaspoon
white fish fillets (e.g. terakihi, snapper, gurnard) 600–700g, cut into 2.5cm chunks
oil (e.g. canola, soy or rice bran) 3 tablespoons
taco shells 12

CHIPOTLE SOUR CREAM

sour cream ½ cup
natural unsweetened Greek yoghurt ½ cup
chipotle sauce 2–4 tablespoons (depending on hotness preference)

MANGO SALSA

tomatoes 3–4, diced
mango 1, peeled and diced
avocado 1 firm ripe, diced
coriander ¾ cup chopped
limes 2, or **lemon** 1, cut into wedges to serve

Per serve
Energy: 2410kj (575 cal)
Carbohydrate: 29.5g
Protein: 32.7g
Fat: 36.5g
Saturated fat: 6.7g

Panko-crumbed Fish 'n' Kumara Chips *with* Coleslaw

I enjoy turning fast food and takeaway dishes into tastier, healthier everyday versions. These fish and chips won't leave you feeling heavy and unhealthy, and will keep the kids happy that they're having a treat!

SERVES: 4–5

PREP TIME: 20–25 MINUTES

COOK TIME: 30–35 MINUTES

KUMARA CHIPS

red kumara 900g–1kg, scrubbed and cut into 2cm–thick chips or wedges
olive oil 2 tablespoons
salt

PANKO–CRUMBED FISH

plain flour 3 tablespoons, seasoned with
salt 1 teaspoon
egg 1, beaten
panko crumbs 1 cup
white fish fillets 4 x 150g boneless, skinless
oil (e.g. canola, soy or rice bran) 2 tablespoons

COLESLAW

cabbage 3 cups, finely shredded
carrots 2 medium, peeled and shredded or grated
spring onions 2, chopped
flat-leaf parsley ¼ cup chopped
creamy dressing ½ cup (see page 252)

TO SERVE

lemon 1, cut into wedges

DAIRY FREE

(Omit yoghurt from dressing)

Per serve
Energy: 2583kj (617 cal)
Carbohydrate: 62.3g
Protein: 37.2g
Fat: 25.3g
Saturated fat: 4.2g

1   Preheat oven to 180°C. Line an oven tray with baking paper. Lay kumara on prepared tray, drizzle over olive oil and toss to coat (using your hands). Season with salt. Bake for 30–35 minutes until crisp and golden.

2   While the chips are cooking, place seasoned flour, beaten egg and panko crumbs on separate plates. Coat each piece of fish first in flour (shaking off any excess), then egg and then panko crumbs. This process makes sure the panko crumbs stick to the fish and you get a nice even coating. Set crumbed fish aside on a dry plate until ready to cook (about 10 minutes before the chips are ready).

3   To make the coleslaw, toss cabbage, carrot, spring onion and parsley with creamy dressing.

4   To cook the fish, heat oil in a large frypan on medium heat. Pan-fry crumbed fish for 2 minutes each side until golden and just cooked through. Add more oil as necessary. You may need to cook the fish in two batches to avoid overcrowding the pan.

5   To serve, place a piece of fish, some chips and coleslaw on each plate. Serve with a wedge of lemon to squeeze over fish just before eating.

Lemon, Caper *and* Parsley-crusted Fish *with* Summer Couscous

If you've never crusted fish before you'll enjoy adding this recipe to your repertoire. This is a quick dish to put together for a light, healthy and delicious dinner with a twist.

SERVES: 4–5

PREP TIME: 15–20 MINUTES

COOK TIME: 10 MINUTES

FISH

dried breadcrumbs ½ cup
lemon finely grated zest of 1
flat-leaf parsley 3 tablespoons finely chopped
capers 1 tablespoon, finely chopped
parmesan cheese 3 tablespoons finely grated
Dijon mustard 1 teaspoon
olive oil 1 tablespoon
white fish fillets (e.g. tarakihi, gurnard, blue cod) 4 x 150g skinless
salt
black pepper freshly ground
olive oil for drizzling

COUSCOUS

courgettes 3–4 medium, peeled into ribbons with a vegetable peeler (discard the inner core of the courgette)
cherry tomatoes 1 punnet
dried couscous ¾ cup
boiling water ¾ cup
salt good pinch
butter knob of
feta 60–70g, crumbled
basil leaves 1 loosely packed cup
lemon 1, cut into wedges, to serve

1 Preheat oven to 200°C. Line 2 oven trays with baking paper. Combine breadcrumbs, lemon zest, parsley, capers and parmesan. Place fish fillets on one of the prepared oven trays. Mix Dijon mustard and olive oil together and spread over each fish fillet, dividing equally. Sprinkle plenty of breadcrumb mixture on top of each fillet, coating well. Season with salt and pepper and drizzle over a little olive oil.

2 Place courgette ribbons and cherry tomatoes on second prepared oven tray. Drizzle with olive oil and season with salt. Place both trays in oven (place fish above vegetables) and bake for 8–9 minutes or until fish is just cooked through.

3 In a bowl, mix couscous with boiling water, salt and butter. Cover and leave to steam for 5 minutes.

4 Fluff up couscous with a fork and toss with cooked cherry tomatoes and courgettes, and feta and basil leaves. To serve, spoon some couscous onto each plate and accompany with a piece of crumbed fish and a lemon wedge to squeeze over.

Per serve
Energy: 1853kj (443 cal)
Carbohydrate: 36.9g
Protein: 37.2g
Fat: 15.3g
Saturated fat: 6.3g

Pan-fried Fish *with* Crouton Salad *and* Gherkin Dressing

Gherkins and crispy croutons make a yummy salad, perfect served with a piece of pan-fried fish. For tips on how to get the skin on your fish nice and crispy, see page 250.

1   Preheat oven to 200°C. Line a baking tray with baking paper. Toss bread cubes with olive oil and parmesan and scatter over prepared baking tray. Season with salt and pepper and cook for 10–15 minutes until golden and crispy.

2   Meanwhile, make the dressing and pan-fry the fish. Combine all dressing ingredients together and set aside. Season fish with salt. Heat butter in a large frypan (preferably non-stick) on medium heat. Cook fish skin side down for 2 minutes, then flip over and continue cooking a further 1–2 minutes until just cooked through. You may need to cook the fish in batches to avoid overcrowding the pan.

3   Toss cherry tomatoes, rocket, red onion and croutons together. To serve, place a piece of fish on each plate and some salad and a lemon wedge to the side. Dress salad with gherkin dressing and serve immediately.

SERVES: 4

PREP TIME: 10–15 MINUTES

COOK TIME: 10–15 MINUTES

CROUTONS

sourdough or **ciabatta bread** 6 slices, cut into 2cm chunks
olive oil 3 tablespoons
parmesan cheese ¼ cup finely grated
salt and **pepper**

DRESSING

mayonnaise ¼ cup
natural unsweetened yoghurt 2–3 tablespoons
Dijon mustard 1 teaspoon
gherkins ¼ cup finely diced
fresh dill 1 tablespoon chopped

FISH AND SALAD

white fish fillets 4 x 150g (skin on)
butter knob of
cherry tomatoes 1 punnet, cut in half
baby rocket 4 good handfuls
red onion ½, thinly sliced
lemon 1, cut into wedges to serve

Per serve
Energy: 2342 kj (560 cal)
Carbohydrate: 25.7g
Protein: 38.5g
Fat: 34.1g
Saturated fat: 9.2g

Fish *with* Fondant Potatoes, Asparagus, Cherry Tomatoes *and* Olive Tapenade

These fondant potatoes are so moreish you're guaranteed to want seconds — the chicken stock makes them really tasty and they caramelise slightly as the stock gets absorbed. This is an impressive and simple dish to serve. If it's not asparagus season, use beans or snow peas instead.

SERVES: 4

PREP TIME: 10 MINUTES

COOK TIME: 30–35 MINUTES

Agria potatoes 4 medium, scrubbed and sliced into 2cm-thick rounds
chicken stock 500ml
salt
rosemary or **thyme** leaves of 1 sprig (optional)
butter 2 tablespoons
olive oil 2 tablespoons
white fish fillets 4 x 150g (skin on)
cherry tomatoes 1 punnet
asparagus 300g, trimmed and halved lengthways
lemon juice of 1
olive tapenade 4 tablespoons (storebought or see page 253)

GLUTEN FREE

Per serve
Energy: 2000kj (478 cal)
Carbohydrate: 31.8g
Protein: 37.3g
Fat: 22.7g
Saturated fat: 7.3g

1 Preheat oven to 220°C. Arrange potatoes in a single layer in a large baking or casserole dish so that they fit snugly. Pour over chicken stock (if using fresh stock, season with salt). Add rosemary or thyme sprig if using, and dot with butter. Bake, uncovered, for 30–35 minutes until potatoes are golden and almost all the stock has been absorbed.

2 Heat olive oil in a large frypan (preferably non-stick) on medium to high heat. Season fish with salt and fry skin side down for 2 minutes until crispy, before flipping over to cook for a further 1–2 minutes, or until just cooked through. You may need to cook the fish in two batches to avoid overcrowding the pan. Remove fish and set aside.

3 Add cherry tomatoes and asparagus to frypan, tossing for 1 minute. Squeeze in lemon juice and cover with a lid (to create steam). Cook for 1–2 more minutes until asparagus is just tender.

4 Briefly warm olive tapenade in microwave for 15–30 seconds. To serve, place some potatoes on each plate, top with a piece of fish, some asparagus and cherry tomatoes and a spoonful of olive tapenade.

Spanish Fish Stew

Chorizo, smoked paprika, tomatoes and capsicum give this easy fish stew a wonderful Spanish flavour. It's delicious served with garlic bread to mop up all the sauce, or alternatively rice cooked with a good pinch of saffron and tossed with a little butter.

1 Heat olive oil in a medium-sized saucepan or large frypan on medium heat. Cook onion, celery, capsicum, chorizo, rosemary and paprika until vegetables are soft, 6–7 minutes.

2 Add crushed tomatoes, stock and chilli flakes if using. Bring to the boil, then lower heat and simmer, uncovered, for 15 minutes to allow stew to thicken slightly. Preheat oven to 180°C to warm the garlic bread.

3 Add lemon juice and fish to the stew, cover and continue cooking for a further 3–4 minutes until fish is just cooked through. Turn off heat and season to taste with salt and pepper.

4 Warm garlic bread in hot oven. To serve, divide stew between shallow bowls, garnish with chopped parsley and accompany with garlic bread.

SERVES: 4

PREP TIME: 10 MINUTES

COOK TIME: 20–25 MINUTES

olive oil 2 tablespoons
onion 1, diced
celery 2 stalks, diced
green capsicum 1, cut into roughly 2cm chunks
red capsicums 2, cut into roughly 2cm chunks
chorizo 2 small firm, sliced
rosemary leaves 1 teaspoon finely chopped
smoked paprika 2 teaspoons
crushed tomatoes 1 x 400g can
fish or **chicken stock** 1 cup
chilli flakes pinch (optional)
lemon juice of ½
firm-fleshed white fish fillets (e.g. trevally, hapuku, monkfish) 500g skinless, cut into 3cm chunks
salt
black pepper freshly ground
garlic bread 8 slices to serve
flat-leaf parsley ¼ cup chopped to garnish

(Gluten-free with rice instead of bread)

Per serve
Energy: 2461kj (588 cal)
Carbohydrate: 35.3g
Protein: 40.0g
Fat: 38.4g
Saturated fat: 15.1g

Harissa Chicken *with* Grape, Mint *and* Pine Nut Tabbouleh

Harissa is a North African spice paste which makes a delicious marinade for chicken and meat. You can buy it pre-made or see page 253 to make your own. Tabbouleh is a fresh and healthy salad using bulghur wheat, which is high in fibre and has a low glycaemic index so is filling while being low in calories.

1   Preheat oven to 220°C. Mix harissa paste with olive oil and smother over chicken legs. If you have the time leave to marinate for 1 hour at room temperature, or up to 24 hours in the fridge, before cooking.

2   Place chicken in a baking dish, season with salt and roast for 25–30 minutes or until cooked through.

3   Place bulghur wheat and a good pinch of salt in a bowl and pour over enough boiling water to cover. Cover and stand for 10–15 minutes until bulghur wheat is tender. Drain off any excess liquid.

4   Toss bulghur wheat with remaining salad ingredients and a few tablespoons of the juices from the cooked chicken. To serve, place a chicken leg on each plate and spoon on some bulghur wheat salad. Accompany with a dollop of Greek yoghurt if desired.

SERVES: 4

PREP TIME: 15 MINUTES

COOK TIME: 25–30 MINUTES

HARISSA CHICKEN

harissa paste 3 tablespoons (storebought or see page 253)
olive oil 2 tablespoons
chicken legs 4 whole (thigh and drum)
salt

BULGHUR WHEAT SALAD

cracked bulghur wheat 1 cup
salt
boiling water enough to cover
grapes 2 cups, halved
red onion 1 small, finely diced
tomatoes 4 small, diced
toasted slivered almonds ½ cup (see page 251)
mint leaves 1 cup, sliced
flat-leaf parsley ½ cup chopped
lemon juice of 1

TO SERVE

natural unsweetened Greek yoghurt (optional)

DAIRY FREE

(Dairy free without yoghurt)

Per serve
Energy: 1985kj (474 cal)
Carbohydrate: 37.5g
Protein: 29.8g
Fat: 22.8g
Saturated fat: 5.0g

Apricot Chicken *with* Mash, Broccoli *and* Almonds

This is an old childhood favourite that my mum used to make. It may seem a bit retro, but classics like this never die. Kids and adults alike will enjoy this meal. It is a handy dish to freeze in portions for those busy nights when you just need to reheat your dinner.

1 Heat olive oil in a large frypan or saucepan on medium heat. Cook onion and garlic until soft, 3–4 minutes.

2 Add chicken, tomato paste, sweet chilli sauce, dried herbs, crushed tomatoes, apricots (including the juice) and chicken stock. Stir, cover and simmer on medium heat for 10 minutes. Remove lid and simmer a further 10–15 minutes, uncovered, or until chicken is cooked through. Stir a few times throughout cooking to prevent sauce catching on the bottom. Season to taste with salt and pepper.

3 Bring a large-sized saucepan of salted water to the boil. While chicken is cooking, cook potatoes in boiling salted water until tender, 10–15 minutes. Drain and mash with butter, milk and salt and pepper to taste.

4 Steam, boil or stir-fry broccoli until bright green and just cooked through, 2–3 minutes. To serve, spoon some mashed potato onto each plate and top with 2–3 chicken thighs or drumsticks, some broccolini or broccoli and scatter over almonds.

SERVES: 4-5

PREP TIME: 15 MINUTES

COOK TIME: 25–30 MINUTES

APRICOT CHICKEN

olive oil 2 tablespoons
onions 2, chopped
garlic 2 cloves, finely chopped
chicken drumsticks or **thighs** 10 skinless
tomato paste 3 tablespoons
sweet chilli sauce 1 tablespoon
mixed dried herbs 1 teaspoon
crushed tomatoes 1 x 400g can
apricot halves in juice 1 x 400g can
chicken stock 1 cup
salt
black pepper freshly ground

MASH

Agria potatoes 800g, peeled and chopped
butter knob of
milk ½ cup

BROCCOLI AND ALMONDS

broccoli 1 head, cut into florets
roasted almonds ¼ cup chopped

(Dairy free without butter and milk)

Per serve
Energy: 2630kj (628 cal)
Carbohydrate: 61.0g
Protein: 39.4g
Fat: 26.5g
Saturated fat: 6.0g

Chicken Schnitzel *with* Potato, Celery *and* Parsley Salad

This dish will become a favourite with the kids — chicken, crunchy coating and good old potato salad. What's not to love? Using panko breadcrumbs gives these schnitzels an extra crispy coating. I like to use a mix of natural yoghurt and mayonnaise for a lighter and healthier but still creamy dressing for the potato salad.

SERVES: 4–5

PREP TIME: 25–30 MINUTES

COOK TIME: 20 MINUTES

CHICKEN SCHNITZEL

chicken breasts 4 boneless, skinless
plain flour 4 tablespoons, seasoned
  with **salt** 1 teaspoon
eggs 2, beaten
panko crumbs 1½ cups
oil (e.g. canola, soy or rice bran)
  2 tablespoons

POTATO, CELERY AND PARSLEY SALAD

baby potatoes 800g (skin on), scrubbed
  and halved
creamy dressing ½ cup (see page 252)
capers 1½ tablespoons, chopped
celery 3–4 stalks, diced
carrots 2, peeled and shredded or grated
parsley ⅓ cup finely chopped

Per serve
Energy: 2247kj (537 cal)
Carbohydrate: 38.5g
Protein: 42.5g
Fat: 24.1g
Saturated fat: 5.6g

1   Preheat oven to 200°C. Butterfly chicken breasts: place a chicken breast flat on a chopping board. Place your hand flat on top of the chicken breast and, using a sharp knife, slice through the chicken breast horizontally, trying to keep an equal thickness on either side. Cut almost to the end (about 5mm from the end), but do not cut all the way through. Open chicken breast out like a book. You now have a butterflied chicken breast! Repeat with remaining breasts.

2   Place seasoned flour, beaten eggs and panko crumbs in separate dishes or plates. Coat each butterflied chicken breast first in flour, then egg, then crumbs. Set aside on a clean, dry plate.

3   Heat oil in a large frypan (preferably non-stick) on medium heat. Pan-fry schnitzel in batches for 1–2 minutes on each side until golden, adding more oil as needed. Transfer schnitzels to an oven tray and bake in oven for a further 10 minutes until chicken is cooked through.

4   Bring a medium-sized saucepan of salted water to the boil. While chicken is in oven, cook potatoes in boiling salted water until tender, 10–12 minutes. Drain.

5   Toss creamy dressing with potatoes, capers, celery, carrot and parsley just before serving. To serve, place a chicken schnitzel on each plate and spoon on some potato salad.

Paprika Chicken *with* Tomatoes, Oregano *and* Pine Nuts *and* Crunchy Garlic Potatoes

You can use either chicken legs or breasts for this recipe — if using breasts they will need only half the time in the oven. The potatoes are twice-cooked to get them really crunchy. Serve with steamed or stir-fried greens or a salad.

SERVES: 4

PREP TIME: 10 MINUTES

COOK TIME: 25–30 MINUTES

CRUNCHY GARLIC POTATOES

Agria potatoes 4 medium (about 800g)
garlic 5–6 cloves, finely chopped
olive oil 3 tablespoons
salt

PAPRIKA CHICKEN

chicken legs or **breasts** 4
smoked paprika 1 heaped teaspoon
olive oil 1 tablespoon
garlic 2 cloves, crushed
lemon finely grated zest
  and juice of 1
pine nuts ¼ cup
cherry tomatoes 2 punnets
balsamic glaze 4 tablespoons
fresh oregano ½ cup chopped

DAIRY FREE   GLUTEN FREE

Per serve
Energy: 2275kj (543 cal)
Carbohydrate: 46.0g
Protein: 50.4g
Fat: 19.5g
Saturated fat: 3.8g

1 Preheat oven to 200°C. Line a large oven tray with baking paper. Prick potatoes in a few places with a fork. Microwave on high for 3–4 minutes or parboil for 6–7 minutes until soft enough for a skewer to go through without any resistance. Roughly chop, then using a fork roughly crush potatoes. Toss crushed potatoes with garlic and olive oil in prepared oven tray and season with salt. Set aside.

2 To make the paprika chicken, rub chicken with smoked paprika and season with salt. Heat olive oil in a large frypan and brown chicken in batches for 2 minutes on both sides. Arrange chicken pieces on oven tray with potatoes and cook for 20–25 minutes until chicken is cooked through and potatoes are crispy and golden.

3 Heat a good drizzle of olive oil in a frypan (you can use the same one the chicken was cooked in) on high heat and add garlic, lemon zest, pine nuts and cherry tomatoes; fry for 2 minutes until the tomato skins are blistered. Turn off heat and add lemon juice, balsamic, oregano and any juices from the cooked chicken. Toss together.

4 To serve, spoon some potatoes onto each plate, follow with a chicken leg, then some tomatoes and juices spooned over the top. Serve with sautéed greens or a salad.

Five-spice Duck, Pomegranate Glaze, Kumara Mash *and* Sesame Spinach

I love cooking duck for special-occasion dinners; it's such a treat. Although most of its fat renders out during cooking, duck should still be kept as an occasional meat because it is still relatively fattier (with the exception of wild duck, which is very lean).

SERVES: 2

PREP TIME: 10 MINUTES

COOK TIME: 30 MINUTES

KUMARA MASH

orange kumara 350–400g, peeled and cut into roughly 2.5cm cubes
butter knob of
milk 3–4 tablespoons
salt
black pepper freshly ground

DUCK AND POMEGRANATE GLAZE

duck breasts 2
Chinese five-spice ¾ teaspoon
pomegranate or **plum juice** ½ cup
brown sugar 1 teaspoon
soy sauce 1 teaspoon
rice vinegar 1 teaspoon

SESAME SPINACH

spinach 2 large handfuls chopped
sesame oil ½ teaspoon

DAIRY FREE   GLUTEN FREE

(Use gluten-free soy sauce)
(Dairy free without milk and butter)

Per serve
Energy: 1820kj (435 cal)
Carbohydrate: 56.8g
Protein: 23.8g
Fat: 12.9g
Saturated fat: 5.7g

1   Preheat oven to 200°C. Bring a medium-sized saucepan of salted water to the boil. Boil kumara in salted water until soft, 10–12 minutes. Drain and mash with butter and milk. Season with salt and pepper. Keep warm.

2   While kumara is cooking, prepare duck breasts. Trim breasts of overhanging fat. Use a sharp knife to score skin (go down to but do not cut through the flesh) at 1cm intervals in a diagonal pattern. Rub five-spice into breasts and season with salt.

3   Heat a large frypan on medium heat. Cook breasts without any oil, skin side down, until golden brown, 3–4 minutes. Most of the fat will render out of the skin. Flip breasts over (so the skin is facing up) and transfer to an ovenproof dish (but do not wash frypan!). Cook in oven for 7–8 minutes or until cooked to medium. Remove from oven and set aside on a plate to rest for 5 minutes.

4   While the duck is in the oven, make the sauce. Pour off most of the liquid fat from the frypan and place pan back on high heat. Add pomegranate or plum juice, brown sugar, soy sauce and rice vinegar. Simmer rapidly, stirring frequently, until reduced to a sauce, 3–5 minutes. Mix in any juices from the resting duck.

5   Heat a drizzle of oil in frypan on medium heat and sauté spinach for 1–2 minutes until wilted. Drizzle over sesame oil.

6   To serve, slice duck breasts on the diagonal. Spoon some kumara mash onto each plate, top with slices of duck breast and some spinach and spoon over sauce.

Shredded Duck, Orange *and* Snow Pea Salad

Asian restaurants do great roast duck that you can buy and take away to use in soups, risottos and salads, like this tasty, minimal effort one that I often throw together when I have guests coming around for a special lunch.

SERVES: 4

PREP TIME: 5–10 MINUTES

COOK TIME: 1½ HOURS IF COOKING DUCK

snow peas 150g
oranges 3, peeled and sliced
cherry tomatoes 1 punnet, halved
roast duck* shredded meat of 1
soy and hoisin dressing ½ cup (see page 252)
toasted sesame seeds 1 tablespoon (see page 251)

DAIRY FREE

Per serve
Energy: 1353kj (323 cal)
Carbohydrate: 15.0g
Protein: 33.4g
Fat: 14.7g
Saturated fat: 3.0g

1 Blanch snow peas by plunging them into boiling water to cook for 1 minute, then drain and plunge into a bowl of iced water (this will ensure they stay nice and crunchy).

2 Toss drained snow peas, orange slices, cherry tomatoes and duck meat together. Just before serving, toss with the dressing and sprinkle over sesame seeds.

*Tip Either buy a roast duck from a Chinese restaurant, or to roast a duck yourself preheat the oven to 180°C, prick duck all over with a sharp knife, season with salt and pepper, and place on a rack in a roasting dish. Roast for 1½ hours, letting all the fat render out

Roast Chicken *with* Preserved Lemon *and* Date Couscous *and* Tahini Yoghurt

You can use chicken breasts instead of legs if you prefer — just cook for half the amount of time. The flavours in this meal are somewhat Middle Eastern, with a lovely balance of sweet, salty and sour.

SERVES: 4

PREP TIME: 10 MINUTES

COOK TIME: 25 MINUTES

ROAST CHICKEN

ground allspice ½ teaspoon
sweet paprika ½ teaspoon
chicken legs 4 whole (thigh and drum)
salt
olive oil 1 tablespoon

COUSCOUS

dried couscous ⅔ cup
boiling water ⅔ cup
spinach or **kale** 2–3 large handfuls chopped
preserved lemon ¼ cup finely chopped
medjool dates 4, chopped, or **dried currants** ¼ cup
roasted almonds ⅓ cup chopped
feta 50–60g, crumbled
mint leaves ½ cup torn
lemon juice to dress
extra virgin olive oil to dress

TAHINI YOGHURT

natural unsweetened thick Greek yoghurt ½ cup
tahini paste 1½–2 tablespoons
garlic 1 clove, minced
lemon juice of ½

1 Preheat oven to 220°C. Rub allspice and paprika into both sides of chicken and season with salt. Heat olive oil in a large frypan on medium heat. Brown chicken, skin side down, in two batches. Transfer to preheated oven to cook for 20–25 minutes or until cooked through.

2 While chicken is roasting, combine couscous, boiling water and ½ teaspoon salt in a bowl, cover and leave to stand for 5 minutes. Fluff up grains with a fork.

3 Heat a drizzle of oil in large frypan and briefly sauté spinach or kale for 1 minute until very lightly wilted. Toss couscous with wilted spinach or kale, preserved lemon, dates or dried currants, almonds, feta and mint. Dress with a squeeze of lemon juice and extra virgin olive oil.

4 Combine yoghurt, tahini, garlic and lemon juice. Season to taste with salt and pepper. To serve, divide couscous between plates and serve with a roast chicken leg to the side and a dollop of tahini yoghurt.

Per serve
Energy: 2491kj (595 cal)
Carbohydrate: 53.5g
Protein: 39.7g
Fat: 25.2g
Saturated fat: 6.8g

Red Duck *and* Pineapple Curry

This delicious curry using duck, fresh pineapple and kaffir lime leaf is a real treat. Simmering the meat for over an hour ensures the duck is nice and tender.

1 Trim duck legs of excess fat and score skin with a sharp knife. Heat a large frypan on medium heat. Season duck with salt and cook with no oil, skin side down, for 8–10 minutes until skin is golden and crispy. Most of the fat should render out from the skin.

2 Set duck legs aside. Pour off most of the liquid fat, leaving about 2 teaspoons in pan. Add shallots and garlic; sauté until golden, 4–5 minutes. Add curry paste and a few tablespoons of coconut milk and cook for 1–2 minutes, stirring constantly with a wooden spoon so paste does not stick to the bottom of pan.

3 Add remaining coconut milk, chicken stock, pineapple, kaffir lime leaves, tomatoes and cooked duck legs to pan. Stir, cover with a tight-fitting lid and lower heat. Simmer for 1 hour 30 minutes until duck is tender, stirring occasionally during cooking. Simmer uncovered for last 15 minutes of cooking. Season to taste with salt.

4 Garnish with coriander and serve with steamed rice and cucumber.

SERVES: 3

PREP TIME: 15–20 MINUTES

COOK TIME: 1 HOUR 30 MINUTES

CURRY AND RICE

duck legs 2
salt
shallots 3, finely chopped
garlic 2 cloves, minced
red curry paste 1–1½ tablespoons
coconut milk ½ x 400g can
chicken stock 2 cups
fresh pineapple 1 cup cubed
kaffir lime leaves 2, central stem removed, sliced
tomatoes 2, chopped

TO SERVE

coriander ½ cup chopped to garnish
steamed rice (see page 251)
cucumber ½, sliced

DAIRY FREE   GLUTEN FREE

Per serve
Energy: 2370kj (566 cal)
Carbohydrate: 71.2g
Protein: 45.9g
Fat: 9.9g
Saturated fat: 4.7g

Hot, Sweet *and* Smoky Grilled Chicken *with* Salsa *and* Coconut Rice

Marinating meat in yoghurt helps tenderise it for a really moist result. If you can, marinate the chicken overnight. For an extra charred and smoky flavour cook it on the barbecue if you've got it going. The coconut rice and mango salsa give a bit of a taste of the Caribbean.

1 Mix yoghurt, brown sugar, smoked paprika, Cajun seasoning or cayenne pepper and garlic together in a large bowl. Add chicken thighs and toss to coat in the marinade. Marinate for at least 3 hours or overnight in the fridge.

2 When ready to cook chicken, preheat oven grill to 230°C or hot. Line an oven tray with baking paper. Place marinated chicken pieces on prepared tray. Season with salt and pepper and drizzle with olive oil. Cook for 15 minutes under hot grill, turning once, until cooked through.

3 To make the salsa, place diced tomato in a bowl and season with a little salt. Leave for a few minutes and then drain the juice that seeps out of the tomatoes. Mix with mango, onion, herbs and jalapeños if using, and season to taste with extra virgin olive oil, lemon juice and salt and pepper.

4 To serve, place two chicken thighs on a plate and spoon over some salsa. Serve with coconut rice and a wedge of lemon to squeeze over just before eating.

SERVES: 4

PREP TIME: 15 MINUTES

MARINATING TIME: 3 HOURS

COOK TIME: 12–15 MINUTES

GRILLED CHICKEN

natural unsweetened yoghurt ¼ cup
brown sugar 2 teaspoons
smoked paprika 2 teaspoons
Cajun seasoning 1 teaspoon, or **cayenne pepper** ½ teaspoon
garlic 2 cloves, minced
chicken thighs 8 boneless, skinless
salt
black pepper freshly ground
olive oil for drizzling

SALSA

tomatoes 4, diced
mango ½ ripe, diced
red onion 1 small, finely diced
coriander or **flat-leaf parsley** ½ cup chopped
pickled jalapeño chillies 1–2, chopped (optional)
extra virgin olive oil to taste
lemon juice to taste

TO SERVE

coconut rice to serve (see page 131)
lemon 1, cut into wedges to serve

GLUTEN FREE

Per serve
Energy: 1162kj (278 cal)
Carbohydrate: 12.0g
Protein: 36.5g
Fat: 9.4g
Saturated fat: 3.0g

Southeast Asian Chicken, Bean *and* Potato Curry

Everyone who has tried this curry has said it's one of the best they've ever had. It's also dead easy to make. Change the vegetable to suit the season: if you don't have beans you could use carrots, courgette or eggplant.

SERVES: 4–5

PREP TIME: 15 MINUTES

COOK TIME: 25 MINUTES

oil (e.g. canola, soy or rice bran) 2 tablespoons
shallots 3, peeled and chopped
garlic 1 clove, finely chopped
ground cumin 1 teaspoon
ground coriander 1 teaspoon
lemongrass 1 stalk, bruised and chopped
kaffir lime leaves 2, central stem removed, sliced
Thai red curry paste 1–1½ tablespoons
brown sugar 1½ tablespoons
coconut cream ⅓ cup
chicken stock 2 cups
crushed tomatoes 1 x 400g can
Agria potatoes 400g, scrubbed and cut into 2.5cm cubes
chicken thighs 8 boneless, skinless
green beans 200g, trimmed

TO SERVE

coriander handful chopped
telegraph cucumber 1, sliced
tomatoes 4, chopped
basmati rice steamed

(Check curry paste is gluten free)

Per serve
Energy: 2510kj (599 cal)
Carbohydrate: 65.0g
Protein: 43.7g
Fat: 18.7g
Saturated fat: 6.0g

1 Heat oil in a large frypan or saucepan on medium heat. Cook shallots and garlic until soft, about 3 minutes. Add cumin, coriander, lemongrass, kaffir lime leaves, curry paste, brown sugar and 1–2 tablespoons of the coconut cream. Cook for 1 minute, constantly stirring with a wooden spoon so the paste does not stick to the bottom of the pan. Add remaining coconut cream and continue to cook for a further 1 minute.

2 Add chicken stock, crushed tomatoes, potatoes and chicken. Bring to the boil, then lower heat to a simmer. Simmer, partially covered, for 15–20 minutes until chicken and potatoes are cooked through. Stir curry occasionally while cooking. Add beans in the last 3 minutes of cooking time.

3 Garnish curry with coriander. Serve curry in a large bowl for everyone to help themselves. Serve with a salad of cucumber and tomato and steamed rice.

Tip If you can't find kaffir lime leaves, use a regular lime leaf or mandarin leaf.

Tandoori Chicken Skewers *with* Lemon, Coconut *and* Almond Pilaf

If time allows, marinate the chicken in the fridge overnight to get the flavours deep inside the meat. This rice tastes fantastic and has a bit of a celebratory feel about it. This is one delicious Indian-inspired meal.

1   Combine chicken with olive oil, lemon juice, tomato paste and tandoori seasoning. If you have time, marinate chicken for an hour, or up to 24 hours, in the fridge.

2   To make the pilaf, heat olive oil in a large-sized saucepan on medium heat and cook onion and garlic until soft and slightly browned, 4–5 minutes. Add turmeric, cinnamon stick, rice, coconut and almonds, and cook, stirring constantly, for 3–4 minutes, coating rice with oil well.

3   Add sultanas, chicken stock, and lemon zest and juice. Stir well and bring to the boil, then reduce to lowest heat and cover with a tight-fitting lid. Leave to cook for 15 minutes on low heat (do not lift lid during cooking). Turn off heat and leave rice, covered (again, do not lift lid), to steam, for a further 8 minutes. Uncover and fluff up rice grains with a fork. Remove cinnamon stick. Keep rice warm.

4   While the rice is cooking, grill the chicken. Preheat oven grill to 200°C or high. Line an oven tray with baking paper. Thread four chicken pieces onto each skewer. Place on prepared tray and season with salt. Cook under hot grill for 6–8 minutes each side or until cooked through.

5   Combine all raita salad ingredients in a bowl. To serve, spoon some pilaf and raita salad onto each plate and accompany with two chicken skewers.

CHICKEN SKEWERS

chicken thighs 8 boneless, skinless, cut into quarters
olive oil 2 tablespoons
lemon juice of 1
tomato paste 2–3 tablespoons
tandoori seasoning 2 heaped teaspoons (storebought or make your own, see page 253)
bamboo skewers 8–10, soaked in water (to prevent burning)
salt

LEMON, COCONUT AND ALMOND PILAF

olive oil 2 tablespoons
onion 1 large, diced
garlic 2 cloves, minced
ground turmeric 1 teaspoon
cinnamon stick 1
long-grain wild rice blend 2 cups
thread coconut ¼ cup
slivered almonds ⅓ cup
sultanas ¾ cup
chicken stock 3½ cups
lemon finely grated zest and juice of 1

RAITA SALAD

natural unsweetened yoghurt 1 cup
carrots 3, shredded or grated
tomatoes 4, diced
mint leaves ½ cup, sliced

(Dairy free without yoghurt)

Per serve
Energy: 3070kj (733 cal)
Carbohydrate: 76.5g
Protein: 41.7g
Fat: 29.7g
Saturated fat: 7.8g

Vietnamese Chicken Noodle Soup

Part of the enjoyment of this dish is loading your soup bowl up with all the different ingredients. Be careful not to overcook the chicken — depending on the size of the breasts, 10–15 minutes in the hot stock is sufficient to ensure they are cooked through but still moist. (To check they are cooked make a small cut with the tip of a sharp knife.)

1. In a large-sized saucepan combine shallots, garlic, lemongrass, ginger, spices, sugar, fish or soy sauce, chicken stock and chicken breasts. Cover with a lid and bring to a gentle boil. As soon as the broth comes to the boil, turn off heat and leave to stand, covered, for 10–15 minutes. This will allow all the flavours to infuse and for the residual heat of the hot stock to cook the chicken breasts.

2. Meanwhile, cook noodles according to packet instructions until just cooked through (do not overcook). Drain and divide between serving bowls.

3. Remove cooked chicken breasts from broth and shred meat using two forks. Set shredded meat aside. Strain soup through a sieve. Return soup to the pan and heat through. Season to taste with more fish or soy sauce and pepper.

4. To serve, ladle hot soup over the noodles, dividing equally among the bowls. Place shredded chicken, carrot, spring onion, red onion, bean sprouts, herbs, chilli if using, and crispy shallots in bowls on the table and allow everyone to help themselves. To eat, top your soup with the condiments and squeeze over a wedge of lime just before eating.

Tip If you have some, add 1 teaspoon of hoisin sauce to each bowl of noodles.

SERVES: 4–5

PREP TIME: 25 MINUTES

COOK TIME: 15 MINUTES

shallots 3, sliced
garlic 3 cloves
lemongrass 1 stalk, chopped
ginger 2.5cm piece, sliced
star anise 3 whole
coriander seeds 1 teaspoon
Chinese five-spice ¼ teaspoon
whole black peppercorns ¼ teaspoon
sugar 1 teaspoon
fish or **soy sauce** 2 tablespoons
chicken stock (unsalted) good-quality fresh, 1.25 litres (5 cups)
chicken breasts 3 boneless, skinless
dried rice stick noodles 300g

TO SERVE

carrot 1, shredded or peeled into ribbons with a vegetable peeler
spring onions 4, sliced
red onion 1 small, thinly sliced
mung bean sprouts 2 large handfuls
coriander 1 large handful chopped
mint leaves 1 handful, chopped
red chilli 1, thinly sliced (optional)
crispy fried shallots 3 tablespoons
lime 1, cut into wedges to serve

DAIRY FREE   GLUTEN FREE

(Use gluten-free soy sauce)

Per serve
Energy: 1790 kj (428 cal)
Carbohydrate: 58.1g
Protein: 33.6g
Fat: 6.9g
Saturated fat: 1.4g

Roast Chicken, Jerusalem Artichokes, Bacon, Brussels Sprouts *and* Gravy

I love Jerusalem artichokes which are delicious when roasted until they are slightly caramelised. They make a good alternative to roast potatoes, and go well with a roast chicken. Preparing Brussels sprouts in this way has converted many sceptics into fans.

SERVES: 5–6

PREP TIME: 15 MINUTES

COOK TIME: 1 HOUR 20 MINUTES

chicken 1 medium (size 14), whole
lemon 1, halved
olive oil for cooking
salt
Jerusalem artichokes 800g, scrubbed and chopped into 2cm pieces
chicken stock fresh ¾ cup
cornflour 1 teaspoon, mixed with **cold water** 1 tablespoon
streaky bacon 3–4 rashers, diced
walnuts ¼ cup roughly chopped
Brussels sprouts 250–300g, stems removed, thinly sliced

DAIRY FREE · GLUTEN FREE

Per serve
Energy: 2101kj (501 cal)
Carbohydrate: 4.9g
Protein: 63.2g
Fat: 25.7g
Saturated fat: 7.4g

1 Preheat oven to 200°C. Line a roasting tray with baking paper (for easy clean-up afterwards). Pat chicken dry and stuff cavity with lemon halves. Rub a little olive oil all over chicken and season well with salt. Place on a rack inside roasting tray and roast for 40 minutes.

2 Take roasting dish out of oven and remove rack with chicken on it. Pour off any roasting juices and reserve to make gravy. Return chicken to roasting tray, without the rack, and scatter Jerusalem artichokes around chicken. Drizzle with a little olive oil and season with salt. Return to oven to roast for a further 30–35 minutes until chicken is cooked through and artichokes are soft and slightly caramelised.

3 When chicken and artichokes are done, remove from oven and leave chicken to rest for 15 minutes while you prepare the gravy and Brussels sprouts. Combine chicken roasting juices, chicken stock and cornflour mixture in a small saucepan and boil for 5 minutes, constantly whisking, until reduced and thickened to a gravy. Keep warm.

4 Heat 1 tablespoon of olive oil in a large frying pan on high heat and cook bacon and walnuts for 2 minutes, then add Brussels sprouts and continue cooking for 4–5 minutes until cooked through and slightly caramelised. Gently toss with the Jerusalem artichokes.

5 To serve, carve chicken and lay pieces on a large platter together with the Jerusalem artichokes, Brussels sprouts, bacon and walnuts. Serve with gravy on the side.

Thyme-crumbed Pork Chops *with* Autumn Salad

The sweetness and crispness of persimmon and pear is well suited to pork. This makes a quick and easy light autumn meal. You can also use thin slices of apple in the salad or if it's summer, the pork is delicious paired with a salad of rocket, stonefruit and blue cheese (see below).

1 Preheat oven to 200°C. Mix panko crumbs, lemon zest, thyme and salt. Coat pork chops or cutlets with crumbs, pressing them on firmly so they stick well to the meat.

2 Heat oil in a large frypan on medium to high heat and cook cutlets in batches for 1–2 minutes on each side until golden brown. Transfer to hot oven and cook for a further 5 minutes until cooked through.

3 Combine all salad ingredients and dress with honey mustard dressing just before serving. To serve, place a crumbed pork chop and some salad on each plate.

Summer Rocket, Stone Fruit *and* Blue Cheese Salad

Toss 4 large handfuls rocket leaves, 2 ripe nectarines or peaches, sliced, and 50–60g blue cheese, crumbled, with a drizzle of honey, balsamic vinegar and extra-virgin olive oil.

SERVES: 4

PREP TIME: 10–15 MINUTES

COOK TIME: 15 MINUTES

CRUMBED PORK CHOPS

panko crumbs 1 cup
lemon finely grated zest of 1
thyme leaves 2 tablespoons finely chopped
salt 1 teaspoon
pork loin chops or **pork cutlets** 4
oil (e.g. canola, soy or rice bran) 1 tablespoon

AUTUMN SALAD

persimmon 1 firm ripe (skin on), thinly sliced
pear 1 firm ripe (skin on), thinly sliced
fennel bulb 1 medium or ½ large, thinly sliced
baby rocket or **spinach** or **soft lettuce** 4 handfuls
walnuts ¼ cup, roughly chopped
honey mustard dressing (see page 253)

DAIRY FREE

Per serve
Energy: 1282kj (306 cal)
Carbohydrate: 18.9g
Protein: 26.4g
Fat: 14.2g
Saturated fat: 2.6g

Chipotle Pulled Pork
Soft Tacos *with* Apple Slaw

There's nothing quite like slow-cooked pork that is so tender it just falls apart. Here it is flavoured with tasty chipotle sauce (chipotles are smoked jalapeño peppers) to create a real Mexican fiesta. Using a dark stout in the sauce gives it a really rich, deep flavour. You could also serve the pulled pork with rice or on top of baked potatoes — delicious!

1   Preheat oven to 160°C. Heat olive oil in a heavy-based flameproof and ovenproof casserole dish, Dutch oven or frypan with a tight-fitting lid. Cook onion until soft and starting to caramelise, 3–4 minutes.

2   Add smoked paprika, pork, chipotle sauce, tomatoes, brown sugar, soy sauce, and stock or stout. Stir, cover with a tight-fitting lid and braise in oven for 1½–2 hours until meat is soft and shreds easily.

3   Remove pork from sauce and use two forks to shred the meat. Boil the sauce (in the dish it was cooked in) on the stove top for 5 minutes or until sauce thickens. Add shredded pork back into the dish and mix together.

4   Mix all slaw ingredients together.

5   To serve, warm tortillas according to packet instructions. Serve shredded pork, slaw, mashed avocado, yoghurt and lime wedges in bowls for everyone to help themselves. Place a good spoonful of pork, slaw, avocado and a dollop of yoghurt in a tortilla, fold up and eat!

SERVES: 4–5

PREP TIME: 25–30 MINUTES

COOK TIME: 1½–2 HOURS' SLOW COOKING

PULLED PORK

olive oil 1 tablespoon
onion 1, diced
smoked paprika 1 teaspoon
pork shoulder 600–700g, cut into 5cm chunks
chipotle sauce 3 tablespoons
crushed tomatoes 1 x 400g can
brown sugar 1 tablespoon
soy sauce 1 tablespoon
beef or **chicken stock** or **stout** 1 cup

APPLE SLAW

green apple 1, sliced and cut into matchsticks
cabbage 1 cup finely shredded
lime juice of 1
carrot 1, shredded or grated
coriander ½ cup chopped

TO SERVE

soft corn tortillas 12 small
avocado 1 ripe, mashed
natural unsweetened thick Greek yoghurt or **sour cream** 1 cup
lime 1, cut into wedges to serve

Per serve
Energy: 3065kj (732 cal)
Carbohydrate: 50.6g
Protein: 38.4g
Fat: 41.6g
Saturated fat: 12.1g

Glazed Pork Fillet, Fried Tomatoes, Celery *and* Beans *with* Tasty Rice

You get a double flavour hit in this recipe by first marinating the pork and then reducing the marinade down to create a delicious sticky glaze. The rice has a few different spices and lemon added to it which makes it a little less ordinary.

SERVES: 4–5

PREP TIME: 10 MINUTES

MARINATING TIME: 15 MINUTES

COOK TIME: 30 MINUTES

PORK AND GLAZE

soy sauce 4 tablespoons
runny honey 2 tablespoons
tomato paste or **tomato sauce**
  3 tablespoons
pork fillet 600g

TASTY RICE

olive oil 1 tablespoon
fennel seeds 1 teaspoon, crushed
cumin seeds 2 teaspoons, crushed
smoked paprika 1 heaped teaspoon
salt ½ teaspoon
lemon juice of 1
long-grain rice 2 cups
water 3 cups

FRIED TOMATOES, CELERY AND BEANS

oil (e.g. canola, soy or rice bran)
  1 tablespoon
garlic 1 large clove, thinly sliced
celery 3–4 stalks, sliced
green beans 250g, trimmed
cherry tomatoes 1 punnet

DAIRY FREE   GLUTEN FREE

(Use gluten-free soy sauce)

Per serve
Energy: 2298kj (549 cal)
Carbohydrate: 72.6g
Protein: 34.8g
Fat: 11.5g
Saturated fat: 2.9g

1   Preheat oven to 220°C. Mix soy sauce, honey and tomato paste or sauce together. Coat pork in glaze and leave to marinate for 15 minutes at room temperature, or overnight in the fridge.

2   While pork is marinating, cook the rice; heat olive oil in a medium-sized saucepan and fry fennel and cumin seeds for 1 minute. Add paprika, salt, lemon juice, rice and water to the pan. Bring to the boil, then as soon as it boils reduce to lowest heat, cover with a tight-fitting lid and cook on lowest heat for 15 minutes (do not remove lid during this time). Turn off heat and leave to steam, still covered (again, don't lift the lid!), for a further 8 minutes.

3   Lift pork out of marinade and place in a casserole or baking dish. Cook in oven for 15–20 minutes, turning once, or until cooked through. Place remaining marinade in a small pan with a splash of water and boil for 2–3 minutes until reduced to a thick glaze (watch carefully so it doesn't burn).

4   Now fry the vegetables. Heat olive oil in a large frypan or wok. Fry garlic for 1 minute, then add celery, green beans and tomatoes. Stir-fry for 3–4 minutes until beans are cooked through.

5   To serve, slice pork fillet on an angle. Spoon some rice and stir-fried vegetables onto each plate, top with pork slices and spoon over glaze.

Barbecued Lamb *and* Olive Panzanella

This is one of those super-tasty barbecue-and-toss-all-together-type meals. If the barbecue is not going, you can cook the lamb and vegetables in a frypan on the stove top. Serve immediately after it is tossed with the dressing, as while you want the croutons to suck up a bit of juice you still want them to retain their texture.

SERVES: 4

PREP TIME: 15 MINUTES

COOK TIME: 10–15 MINUTES

olive oil 2–3 tablespoons
lamb backstraps or **leg steaks** 600g
salt
sourdough or **ciabatta bread*** 6 thick
   slices, roughly torn into 2.5cm chunks
asparagus 1 bunch, washed, ends
   trimmed and halved

TO ASSEMBLE

black olives ½ cup
vine tomatoes 6 medium ripe, chopped
roast red capsicum 1 (from a jar), sliced
red onion ½ small, sliced
basil leaves large handful
red wine vinegar dressing ½ cup (see
   page 252)

DAIRY
FREE

Per serve
Energy: 1971kj (471 cal)
Carbohydrate: 32.3g
Protein: 18.6g
Fat: 30.2g
Saturated fat: 5.3g

1 Heat barbecue hot plate to medium to high. Rub 1 tablespoon of the olive oil over lamb and season with salt. Cook lamb for 1–2 minutes on each side for medium rare or until cooked to your liking. Remove meat and set aside on a plate to rest for 5 minutes, reserving any juices.

2 Meanwhile, toss remaining olive oil with bread chunks (using your hands) and fry on the barbecue hot plate for a few minutes, turning once, until golden. Season with a little salt.

3 Wash asparagus, shake off excess water, and add to hot plate. Cook asparagus for 1–2 minutes until just cooked.

4 Slice lamb on an angle. Just before serving, toss with reserved juices, asparagus, toasted bread, olives, tomatoes, capsicum, onion, basil leaves and dressing. Serve immediately.

*Tip Bread that's a few days old is best for this salad.

Salsa Verde Lamb Cutlets *with* Roast Tomatoes, Spinach *and* Cannellini Beans

This dish is full of goodness, with lamb high in iron, beans high in fibre, tomatoes high in lycopene and spinach high in folate. You can blend the salsa verde in a food processor or blender; however, I prefer to finely chop all the ingredients to retain a bit of texture.

1 Preheat oven to 200°C and line an oven tray with baking paper. Mix all salsa verde ingredients together. Rub half of salsa verde all over lamb rack and reserve remaining salsa verde.

2 Place lamb rack and whole cherry tomatoes on prepared oven tray. Season lamb and tomatoes with salt, and roast for 20 minutes for medium-rare lamb — if you like your meat more well done, roast a further 3–5 minutes. Rest lamb for 10 minutes before slicing between cutlets.

3 Gently toss cannellini beans with roast tomatoes and remaining salsa verde. Season to taste with salt and pepper.

4 Just before serving, heat a drizzle of olive oil in a frypan on medium heat and stir-fry spinach until wilted, about 1 minute. To serve, spoon some beans, tomatoes and spinach onto each plate and top with 2–3 lamb cutlets. Spoon over any juices from the resting lamb.

Tip For perfectly cooked lamb rack, the oven must be very hot and the meat needs to rest for at least half its cooking time before slicing. Cover with tinfoil and tea towels to keep meat warm while resting.

SERVES: 2–3

PREP TIME: 15 MINUTES

COOK TIME: 20 MINUTES

SALSA VERDE

flat-leaf parsley ¾ cup very finely chopped
thyme leaves 1 tablespoon very finely chopped
capers 1 tablespoon, finely chopped
garlic 1 clove, minced
anchovy fillets 2, finely chopped (optional)
lemon juice 2 tablespoons
Dijon mustard 1 teaspoon
extra virgin olive oil 3 tablespoons

LAMB, TOMATOES AND BEANS

lamb rack 1 (8 cutlets), trimmed of fat cap
cherry tomatoes 1 punnet
salt
cannellini beans 1 x 400g can, rinsed and drained
black pepper freshly ground
baby spinach 150–200g

DAIRY FREE   GLUTEN FREE

Per serve
Energy: 2584kj (617 cal)
Carbohydrate: 20.5g
Protein: 55.3g
Fat: 36.0g
Saturated fat: 10.8g

Venison, Beetroot *and* Hazelnut Salad

Venison is a very lean meat and very high in iron. Because it is so lean, avoid cooking it any more than to medium or it will become tough. For best results, make sure your meat is at room temperature before cooking and rest it for at least 5–10 minutes before slicing. This is another nutrient-packed dish, with beetroot and rocket high in antioxidants and hazelnuts full of healthy monounsaturated fats.

1 Preheat oven to 180°C. Line an oven tray with baking paper. Toss beetroot with maple syrup or honey and 1 tablespoon of olive oil. Place on prepared tray and roast for 20–25 minutes until soft.

2 Heat remaining olive oil in a frypan. Season venison with salt and cook for 2 minutes on each side for medium-rare (do not cook more than medium). Rest venison for 5–10 minutes before slicing on an angle.

3 To serve, toss beetroot and venison slices with remaining ingredients and divide between plates.

SERVES: 2–3

PREP TIME: 10 MINUTES

COOK TIME: 25 MINUTES

beetroot 2 medium, peeled and cut into 1.5cm-thick wedges
maple syrup or **runny honey** 1 tablespoon
olive oil 2 tablespoons
venison backstrap 1 x 300g (approx.), or **medallions** 4 x 70g (approx.)
salt
roasted hazelnuts ⅓ cup, chopped
baby rocket leaves 2 large handfuls
red onion ½ small, thinly sliced
feta 40–50g, crumbled
balsamic glaze 1½ tablespoons
extra virgin olive oil 2 tablespoons

GLUTEN FREE

Per serve
Energy: 2140kj (511 cal)
Carbohydrate: 15.4g
Protein: 31.7g
Fat: 37.6g
Saturated fat: 7.6g

Lamb *with* Tzatziki *and* Roast Cauliflower Pearl Couscous

Tzatziki is a refreshing cucumber, mint and yoghurt accompaniment that is delicious with meat and chicken. Quite different to the more common instant couscous, pearl couscous is, in fact, small toasted pasta. It is sometimes called Israeli couscous and is great in salads, soups and stews.

SERVES: 4–5

PREP TIME: 20 MINUTES

COOK TIME: 20 MINUTES

TZATZIKI

telegraph cucumber ½, grated
salt
natural unsweetened Greek yoghurt
 ½ cup
mint leaves ⅓ cup sliced
lemon juice of ½

ROAST CAULIFLOWER PEARL COUSCOUS

cauliflower or **broccoflower** 1 small,
 chopped into florets
onion 1, chopped
olive oil 2–3 tablespoons
cumin seeds 1 teaspoon, crushed
rosemary leaves 1 tablespoon,
 finely chopped
pearl or **Israeli couscous** 2 cups
chicken stock 2¼ cups
kalamata olives ½ cup, roughly chopped
 (optional)

LAMB

olive oil 1 tablespoon
lamb leg steaks 4 x 150g

Per serve
Energy: 2212kj (528g)
Carbohydrate: 46.7g
Protein: 25.0g
Fat: 27.0g
Saturated fat: 7.1g

1 Preheat oven to 200°C. To make the tzatziki, mix grated cucumber with a good pinch of salt. Place in a sieve over a bowl and set aside for 5 minutes to allow the salt to draw out water from the cucumber. Squeeze out excess water from cucumber using clean hands. Mix with yoghurt, mint and lemon juice. Set aside.

2 Toss cauliflower or broccoflower and onion with olive oil, cumin and rosemary on an oven tray. Season with salt and roast for 20–25 minutes until lightly browned but cauliflower still has a bit of texture.

3 Combine couscous and chicken stock in a saucepan and bring to the boil. Lower heat and simmer for 10 minutes, partially covered with a lid, stirring occasionally, until chicken stock is absorbed and couscous is al dente (just cooked). Cover and leave to steam a further 5 minutes. Toss couscous with roast cauliflower and kalamata olives if using.

4 To cook the lamb, heat olive oil in a large frypan. Season lamb with salt and cook for 2 minutes on each side for medium-rare, or until cooked to your liking. Rest for a few minutes before slicing on an angle. To serve, spoon some couscous and tzatziki onto each plate and top with slices of lamb.

Lamb Ratatouille *with* Polenta *and* Gremolata

This is a quick stew using lamb leg steak, so it doesn't have to cook for hours to be tender. It is delicious with creamy polenta and gremolata, a condiment of parsley, garlic and lemon which adds a zesty hit of freshness.

SERVES: 4–5

PREP TIME: 15 MINUTES

COOK TIME: 25–30 MINUTES

LAMB RATATOUILLE

lamb leg steak 800g, cut into 2.5cm chunks
plain flour 2 tablespoons, mixed with **salt** 1 teaspoon
olive oil 2 tablespoons
red onion 1, cut into 1cm-thick wedges
courgette 1, cut into 1cm-thick slices
eggplant 1, cut into 2.5cm cubes
red capsicum 1, cut into 1cm-thick slices
crushed tomatoes 1 x 400g can
beef or **chicken stock** 2 cups
salt
black pepper freshly ground

POLENTA

chicken stock 4 cups
polenta ⅔ cup, instant or quick cooking
parmesan cheese 1 cup grated
flat-leaf parsley ¼ cup chopped

TO SERVE

gremolata 3 tablespoons (see page 253)

(Gluten-free with cornflour instead of flour)

Per serve
Energy: 2194kj (524 cal)
Carbohydrate: 34.2g
Protein: 48.0g
Fat: 22.3g
Saturated fat: 8.8g

1 Coat lamb pieces in seasoned flour. Heat olive oil in a large frypan on high heat. Brown lamb in two batches for 2 minutes each side (browning in batches will ensure a nice even browning of the meat and avoid it stewing in the pan). Set browned lamb aside.

2 Add onion, courgette, eggplant and capsicum to the hot pan with a drizzle of olive oil. Cook the vegetables on high heat to get them a bit charred, 5–6 minutes.

3 Add crushed tomatoes, stock and cooked lamb. Simmer, uncovered, for 15–20 minutes on medium heat until sauce has slightly reduced. Season to taste with salt and pepper.

4 Meanwhile, make the polenta. Five to 10 minutes before the lamb ratatouille is ready, bring chicken stock to the boil in a saucepan. Add polenta in a stream, while stirring continuously with a wooden spoon. Continue stirring for 5 minutes until polenta starts to thicken and is the consistency of porridge. Turn off the heat and fold through parmesan cheese and parsley. To serve, place some polenta onto each plate and top with lamb ratatouille and a spoonful of gremolata.

Sausage *and* Three Sisters Penne Pasta

Sausages and pasta are a comfort-food combination that I'll never tire of. The key to this recipe is using good-quality sausages. They have to be raw as the meat is squeezed out and fried, giving it a crumbly texture. If you're wondering what 'three sisters' means, it simply refers to onion, carrot and celery — the three vegetables that inherently go together.

SERVES: 4–5

PREP TIME: 10 MINUTES

COOK TIME: 25–30 MINUTES

pork sausages good-quality raw 600g
olive oil 1 tablespoon
dried penne pasta 400g
fennel seeds 1 tablespoon
garlic 2 cloves, chopped
onion 1, diced
celery 4 stalks, diced, reserving leaves to garnish
carrot 1 large, peeled and diced
tomato paste ¼ cup
crushed tomatoes 2 x 400g cans
sugar 1 teaspoon
salt
black pepper freshly ground
parmesan cheese 60g, grated
flat-leaf parsley ½ cup chopped

Per serve
Energy: 2833kj (676 cal)
Carbohydrate: 72.7g
Protein: 28.1g
Fat: 30.8g
Saturated fat: 11.8g

1 Bring a large saucepan of salted water to the boil to cook pasta. Snip off the ends of the sausage casings and squeeze out the raw soft sausage meat.

2 Heat olive oil in a large frypan on medium to high heat. Add raw sausage meat and fry for 5 minutes until almost cooked through. Use a wooden spoon to roughly break up meat, leaving some bits more chunky than others.

3 Add pasta to boiling water and cook until al dente, about 10 minutes.

4 Add fennel seeds, garlic, onion, celery and carrot to pan and fry with sausage meat for a further 5 minutes until garlic, onion and celery are soft. Add tomato paste, canned tomatoes and sugar. Simmer for 10–12 minutes until sauce has thickened. Season to taste with salt and pepper.

5 Drain pasta and add back to the pan, along with tomato and sausage sauce. Mix together. To serve, spoon some pasta and sauce into each bowl and garnish with parmesan cheese and chopped parsley and celery leaves.

Beef, Eggplant *and* Ricotta Lasagne

This is a clever lasagne because it packs in vegetables without anyone noticing, and you don't even have to make a white sauce; instead ricotta is used between the layers. I find this very handy to freeze in portions for a quick dinner served with a side salad. If you wanted to make this a gluten-free lasagne, simply use more slices of eggplant in place of the pasta sheets.

1 Preheat oven to 180°C. Line 2 baking trays with baking paper. Arrange eggplant slices on prepared baking trays, drizzle over 3 tablespoons of olive oil and season with salt. Bake for 15 minutes until soft and lightly browned.

2 Heat remaining 2 tablespoons of olive oil in a large frypan or saucepan on medium heat. Sauté onions and garlic until soft, 3–4 minutes. Add beef mince and cook for 5 minutes, stirring to break up mince. Add tomato paste, crushed tomatoes, oregano and sugar. Bring to the boil, then lower heat and simmer, uncovered, for 10–15 minutes until sauce has thickened. Season to taste with salt and pepper.

3 Mix ricotta and 1 cup of grated cheese. To assemble the lasagne, spread ½ cup of ricotta mixture on the base of a large square or rectangular baking dish. Lay a sheet or sheets of lasagne on top (you may need to cut the lasagne sheets to fit), then pour over 2 cups of tomato and mince sauce to cover evenly. Arrange half of the eggplant slices on top, slightly overlapping. Spoon ¾ cup of ricotta mixture on top of eggplant. Cover with another sheet of lasagne. Repeat process once more so that you have two full layers of mince, eggplant and ricotta, ending with a final layer of lasagne on top. Spread with remaining ricotta mixture and sprinkle over extra grated cheese. Bake in oven for 30–35 minutes until cheese is melted and bubbly on top.

4 Stand lasagne for 10–15 minutes before serving (this will allow it to set so that it is not too sloppy when you cut into it). Serve with a simple tomato and lettuce salad.

SERVES: 6

PREP TIME: 25 MINUTES

COOK TIME: 1 HOUR

eggplants 2 large, sliced into 1cm-thick rounds
olive oil 5 tablespoons
salt
onions 2 medium, diced
garlic 2 cloves, finely chopped
lean beef mince 400g
tomato paste ½ cup
crushed tomatoes 2 x 400g cans
dried oregano 1 teaspoon
sugar 1 teaspoon
black pepper freshly ground
ricotta cheese soft 500g
cheese (e.g. cheddar, edam or colby) 1 cup grated + extra ¼ cup for sprinkling
fresh lasagne 3–4 large sheets, or **dried lasagne** 10–12 smaller sheets

Per serve
Energy: 2582kj (617 cal)
Carbohydrate: 32.1g
Protein: 38.0g
Fat: 35.4g
Saturated fat: 14.9g

Sizzling Sherry *and* Black Pepper Beef Hot Plate

You'll feel like you're in a Chinese restaurant when you serve this steaming and sizzling away to the table. You will need a heavy cast-iron pan, grill or hot plate, as the dish needs to get up to a very high temperature to be able to retain its heat. The residual heat of the hot plate cooks the meat and vegetables through. The combination of black pepper and sweet sherry gives it an amazing flavour.

1 Season steaks with salt. Heat oil in a frypan on high heat and brown steaks, 1 minute on each side, leaving the middle of the steaks rare. Leave steaks to rest for 5 minutes before slicing into thin strips on an angle.

2 Toss onion, garlic, ginger, capsicum and beef slices together.

3 Combine sherry, soy sauce, cornflour, sesame oil and pepper in a small bowl. Heat in microwave for 30–60 seconds or on stove top.

4 When ready to serve, heat a large cast-iron frypan, dish, sizzling or grill plate until very, very hot, either on the stove top or in the oven. (You will need to heat it for at least 5 minutes on very high heat.) Add beef and vegetables to the hot plate, stir briefly around plate then pour over sherry mixture — it will bubble rapidly. Garnish with spring onions and immediately bring to the table, sizzling hot. Mix meat and vegetables around the hot plate to cook further. Serve with steamed rice.

Tip Be careful not to burn yourself — use oven mitts or thickly folded tea towels to carry the hot plate to the table and set it down on a suitable surface (either a heat-resistant tile or placemat or a few tea towels stacked up).

SERVES: 4–5

PREP TIME: 15 MINUTES

COOK TIME: 10 MINUTES

lean beef steak (e.g. Scotch, rump or sirloin) 400–500g (at room temperature)
salt
oil (e.g. canola, soy or rice bran) 1 tablespoon
onion 1, thinly sliced
garlic 2 cloves, chopped
ginger 2.5cm piece, peeled and cut into thin matchsticks
red or **green capsicums** 2, thinly sliced
sherry ½ cup
soy sauce 3 tablespoons
cornflour 1 teaspoon
sesame oil 2 teaspoons
black pepper 1½ teaspoons, freshly ground

TO SERVE

spring onions 1 bunch, thinly sliced
plain steamed rice (see page 251)

(Use gluten-free soy sauce)

Per serve
Energy: 2137kj (510 cal)
Carbohydrate: 57.0g
Protein: 29.8g
Fat: 15.0g
Saturated fat: 4.5g

Lebanese Lamb Pizza *with* Carrot Salad

Lebanese flat bread (similar to a large pita bread) makes a great pizza base that's lighter and healthier, and crisps up really nicely in the oven. I like to make up this spiced tomato sauce in bulk to freeze in portions, ready for a delicious pizza I can put together in less than 15 minutes.

1 Preheat oven to 200°C. Heat olive oil in a medium frypan on medium heat. Cook onion and garlic until soft, 3–4 minutes. Stir in cumin, coriander, chilli powder if using, tomato paste and crushed tomatoes. Simmer for 8–10 minutes until thick and jam-like. Set aside.

2 Season lamb with salt. Heat a drizzle of olive oil in a frypan on high heat and fry lamb 1–2 minutes on each side for medium-rare or until cooked to your liking. Set aside to rest for 5–10 minutes before slicing on an angle.

3 Place flat breads on a baking tray. Spread with spiced tomato sauce and sprinkle over onion, cheese, pine nuts and feta. Cook in oven for 8–10 minutes until edges are crispy and cheese is melted.

4 Combine carrot and coriander with lemon juice. To serve, top pizza with slices of lamb, dollop over Greek yoghurt, sprinkle over sumac if using and serve with carrot salad.

SERVES: 4

PREP TIME: 10 MINUTES

COOK TIME: 25–30 MINUTES

SPICED TOMATO SAUCE

olive oil 1 tablespoon
onion ½, diced
garlic 1 clove, chopped
ground cumin 1 heaped teaspoon
ground coriander 1 heaped teaspoon
chilli powder 1 teaspoon (optional)
tomato paste 1 heaped tablespoon
crushed tomatoes ½ x 400g can

BREAD BASE AND TOPPINGS

lamb leg steaks 2 (approximately 300g)
salt
Lebanese flat bread 2 large
red onion 1 small or ½ medium, thinly sliced
cheese (e.g. mozzarella or edam) 1 cup grated
pine nuts ¼ cup
feta 50g, crumbled
natural unsweetened thick Greek yoghurt ⅓ cup
sumac 1 teaspoon (optional)

CARROT SALAD

carrots 2–3, peeled and shredded or peeled into ribbons with a vegetable peeler
coriander ¾ cup roughly chopped
lemon juice of ½

Per serve
Energy: 2357 kj (564 cal)
Carbohydrate: 32.3g
Protein: 38.6g
Fat: 30.7g
Saturated fat: 14.3g

Open Red Wine Beef Pie *with* Baby Vegetables

This is a delicious, comforting winter pie, made a bit lighter by having just a pastry top. Here, the stew is cooked slowly on a very low heat on the stove top, but you can also cook it in a covered casserole dish in the oven at 160°C for 2 hours, or in a slow cooker. Either way, slow cooking on low heat will guarantee tender beef.

1   Dust beef chunks in seasoned flour. Heat olive oil in a heavy-based, deep frypan or saucepan, with a tight-fitting lid, on medium to high heat. Brown beef pieces, about 1 minute each side, in two batches, then set aside.

2   Add onion to the pan and cook until soft, 3–4 minutes. Add wine and bring to the boil. Rub the bottom of the pan with a wooden spoon to release any pan brownings into the liquid. Add tomato paste, beef stock, thyme sprigs, browned meat and any juices to the pan. Lower heat and cover with a lid. Simmer on very low heat for 2 hours until beef is tender. Make sure it does not come to a boil at any time. Remove lid and simmer for a further 15 minutes.

3   Preheat oven to 200°C. Cut out four 9cm x 9cm squares of pastry from the sheet. Lay on a baking tray and bake for 10–15 minutes until pastry is puffed and golden.

4   Steam or boil carrots and peas until just tender, 4–6 minutes. To serve, spoon some beef stew and vegetables onto each plate, and top with a square of puff pastry.

SERVES: 4

PREP TIME: 15–20 MINUTES

COOK TIME: 15 MINUTES + 2 HOURS' SLOW COOKING

beef blade or **chuck steak** 600–700g, cut into 2.5cm chunks
flour 2 tablespoons, seasoned with **salt** 1 teaspoon
olive oil 2 tablespoons
onion 1, diced
red wine 1 cup
tomato paste 2 tablespoons
beef stock 1 cup
thyme 2–3 sprigs
puff pastry 1 square sheet
baby carrots 12–16, peeled
frozen baby peas 2 cups

DAIRY FREE

Per serve
Energy: 2066kj (493cal)
Carbohydrate: 28.3g
Protein: 39.5g
Fat: 19.7g
Saturated fat: 7.9g

Gourmet Steak Sandwich *with* Caramelised Onions *and* Horseradish Crème Fraîche

These gourmet steak sandwiches are a real crowd-pleaser and quick and easy to make. The caramelised onions can be used as a flavour booster in many other dishes — in soups, casseroles, tarts, on pizza, the list goes on — they are incredibly useful and will keep in the fridge for up to a week.

SERVES: 4

PREP TIME: 10 MINUTES

COOK TIME: 15 MINUTES

CARAMELISED ONIONS

olive oil 2 tablespoons
onions 2 large, sliced
brown sugar 2 teaspoons
balsamic vinegar 1½ tablespoons

STEAK SANDWICH

beef Scotch fillet steak 4 x 120–150g (at room temperature)
salt
sourdough bread 8 slices
crème fraîche ⅓ cup
horseradish sauce 2 teaspoons
tomato chutney ⅓ cup
tomatoes 2, sliced
cos lettuce leaves large handful
avocado 1 firm ripe, sliced

Per serve
Energy: 2734kj (653 cal)
Carbohydrate: 41.8g
Protein: 37.0g
Fat: 36.9g
Saturated fat: 13.4g

1 To make the caramelised onions, heat olive oil in a medium or large frypan on medium heat. Cook onion until soft and lightly browned, 5–6 minutes. Add brown sugar and balsamic vinegar, and continue cooking for 2 minutes until onions are thick and slightly jammy.

2 Drizzle a little olive oil in a frypan on high heat. Season steaks with salt and pan-fry for 2 minutes on each side for medium-rare, or until cooked to your liking. Rest steak for 5 minutes before slicing on an angle.

3 Lightly toast sourdough in toaster (or oven preheated to 180°C) for a few minutes. Mix crème fraîche with horseradish.

4 To serve, spread crème fraîche and tomato chutney on two slices of toasted sourdough. Layer caramelised onions, steak slices, tomato, lettuce leaves and avocado on top. Top with another slice of toasted sourdough. Alternatively, you can enjoy this as a lighter open sandwich and serve one slice of sourdough per person with fillings piled on top.

Steak *with* Orange Miso Sauce, Sesame Cavolo Nero *and* Kumara Mash

This sauce will leave you licking your plate. You could also use silverbeet, chard, kale or spinach instead of cavolo nero, and swede instead of kumara. Cavolo nero is a dark green leafy vegetable that is becoming increasingly popular, which is great as it is full of folate and other vitamins and minerals. See page 250 for tips on how to cook steak.

1 Bring a medium-sized saucepan of salted water to the boil. Cook kumara in boiling salted water until soft, 10–15 minutes. Drain and mash with butter and milk. Season to taste with salt and pepper. Set aside and keep warm.

2 While kumara is boiling, cook the steaks. Heat a drizzle of olive oil in a frypan or griddle on high heat. Season steaks with a little salt (but not too much as the miso sauce will be quite salty) and cook in batches for 2 minutes on each side for medium-rare, or until cooked to your liking. Set steaks aside to rest for 5 minutes while you make the sauce. Keep the frypan on the heat.

3 Mix miso and orange juice together and add to hot pan. Bring to the boil and allow to boil rapidly for 5–7 minutes until reduced to a sauce. Add any resting juices from the steak to the pan.

4 To cook the cavolo nero, heat olive oil in a large frypan. Add leaves and sesame oil. Stir-fry until leaves are wilted, 1–2 minutes. Add sesame seeds and toss with the greens.

5 To serve, slice steaks on an angle. Spoon some mash onto each plate, top with cavolo nero, slices of steak and spoon over some orange miso sauce.

SERVES: 4

PREP TIME: 5 MINUTES

COOK TIME: 15–20 MINUTES

KUMARA MASH

orange kumara 700g (about 1½ large kumara), peeled and chopped
butter knob of
milk 4–5 tablespoons
salt
black pepper freshly ground

STEAK AND SAUCE

olive oil for cooking
beef Scotch fillet steaks 4 x 120–150g (at room temperature)
white miso paste 2 tablespoons
orange juice 1½ cups, sieved to remove pulp

SESAME CAVOLO NERO

olive oil 1 tablespoon
cavolo nero 150g, tough stems removed, leaves chopped
sesame oil 1 teaspoon
toasted sesame seeds 2 teaspoons

DAIRY FREE   GLUTEN FREE

(Dairy free without butter and milk)

Per serve
Energy: 2333kj (557 cal)
Carbohydrate: 56.0g
Protein: 32.1g
Fat: 23.2g
Saturated fat: 8.3g

lighter desserts

Dessert is one of life's greatest pleasures. Unfortunately they're often high in fat and sugar. While you needn't worry about this on special occasions, if you feel like something sweet a bit more often then I find the best solution is not to deny yourself, but rather have something sweet that is also healthy.

Fruit-based desserts are great for satisfying your sweet tooth as well as counting towards your fruit intake. Home-made fruit sorbets, ice-creams and fruit puddings are an excellent way to get more fruit into your day while seeing to that craving for 'a little something extra'. They're perfect for getting fruit into kids, in particular — they won't think twice that the treat they're having is actually good for them!

This section makes the most of nature's original sweet treat, with tempting seasonal fruit-based desserts, from my mandarin syrup cake that is gluten and dairy free and has no added fat (yet is as moist and delicious as dessert cakes get) to grilled peaches with berry sauce and pistachio crumble topping. Other desserts, such as my coconut vanilla yoghurt panna cotta, are creamy and decadent, but with half the calories you'd expect. These desserts are sweet, satisfying and delicious, yet are light enough that they won't leave you feeling heavy and over full — which I think is the perfect way to end dinner!

Mandarin Syrup Cake

This is an incredibly clever cake — it's gluten free, dairy free and has no added fat (no oil or butter), yet is as moist and delicious as cakes get. It uses whole fruit boiled until soft and then you blitz it up (skin, pith and all), which gives the cake its amazing mandarin flavour and texture. It keeps well for up to a week in the fridge, can be frozen, and can be eaten cold or warm.

1 Place whole mandarins in a large saucepan and cover with plenty of cold water. Cover with a lid and boil gently for 1½ hours. Drain and allow mandarins to cool slightly.

2 Preheat oven to 180°C. Grease and line a 21cm round springform cake tin with baking paper. Remove the stem end of the mandarins, then cut in half and remove any pips. Place fruit (skin, pith, flesh and all) in a food processor or blender and blitz until smooth. Add all other cake ingredients and blitz until well combined.

3 Pour into prepared cake tin and bake for 1 hour or until a skewer inserted in the middle of the cake comes out clean. Cover cake with tinfoil halfway through cooking time to avoid the top browning too much. Remove cake from oven and leave in the tin while you make the syrup.

4 Mix sugar, mandarin and lime juice together and pour over cake while warm. Allow cake to cool slightly before removing from tin. The cake is nice served warm or cold with Greek yoghurt or crème fraîche.

*Tip If you don't have mandarins, instead use the same weight of small tangelos for the cake and 1 tangelo for the syrup.

SERVES: 10

PREP TIME: 10 MINUTES + 1½ HOURS TO BOIL MANDARINS

COOK TIME: 1 HOUR

mandarins* 330–370g (3–6 whole mandarins, depending on size)
blanched ground almonds 200g
white sugar 1 cup
eggs 5
vanilla extract or **essence** 1 teaspoon
baking powder 1 teaspoon

SYRUP

sugar ¼ cup
mandarin juice of 1
lime juice of 1
natural unsweetened Greek yoghurt or **crème fraîche** to serve

DAIRY FREE   GLUTEN FREE

(Check baking powder is gluten free)
(Dairy free without yoghurt or crème fraîche)

Per serve
Energy: 1254kj (299 cal)
Carbohydrate: 32.8g
Protein: 8.9g
Fat: 14.9g
Saturated fat: 3.0g

Stone Fruit Tarts

These delightful little tarts are such a joy to make and eat in the peak of summer when stone fruit is bountiful. Cut the pastry to different sizes to fit the shape of the different fruits — so cute!

MAKES: 12 SMALL TARTS

PREP TIME: 15 MINUTES

COOK TIME: 15 MINUTES

puff pastry 2 x 24cm sheets
apricots 2 ripe, halved and stoned
nectarines or **peaches** 2 ripe, halved and stoned
plums 2 ripe, halved and stoned
runny honey ¼ cup + extra for drizzling
natural unsweetened thick Greek yoghurt to serve

Per serve
Energy: 390kj (93 cal)
Carbohydrate: 11.5g
Protein: 1.4g
Fat: 4.7g
Saturated fat: 2.9g

1   Cut out 12 circles (8–9cm diameter) of pastry using a scone cutter or a glass.

2   Cut a criss-cross into the cut side of the fruit halves, and push down edges to flatten fruit slightly. Place fruit halves, cut side up, on pastry rounds and drizzle over ¼ cup honey.

3   Bake in oven for 15 minutes until pastry is puffed and golden and fruit is soft. Drizzle with more honey and serve with a dollop of Greek yoghurt on the side.

Tropical Fruit Carpaccio *with* Mint *and* Coconut Sugar

Thin slivers of tropical fruit with a squeeze of tangy lime and a sprinkle of mint and coconut sugar make a simple delicious dessert that's light on calories.

SERVES: 4

PREP TIME: 15 MINUTES

pineapple ½ ripe, cut lengthways
mango 1 ripe
papaya ½ ripe

MINT AND COCONUT SUGAR

mint leaves ½ cup, sliced
lime finely grated zest of 1
sugar ¼ cup
toasted thread coconut ¼ cup
lime 1, cut into wedges to serve

DAIRY FREE   GLUTEN FREE

Per serve
Energy: 780kj (186 cal)
Carbohydrate: 36.0g
Protein: 1.8g
Fat: 4.2g
Saturated fat: 3.4g

1   Slice 1–2cm off the top and bottom of the half pineapple so that it stands upright on a chopping board. Use a sharp knife to remove the skin, then cut in half lengthways again (so you have two large wedges) and slice off the tough core. Slice pineapple very thinly lengthways. Peel mango and papaya and slice flesh very thinly. Arrange fruit on serving plates.

2   Place mint leaves, lime zest and 2–3 teaspoons of the sugar in a mortar and pestle and bash to a paste. Use a teaspoon to mix in the remaining sugar and toasted coconut.

3   Sprinkle mint and coconut sugar over fruit and serve with a lime wedge to squeeze over just before eating.

Banana *and* Pistachio Cigars

These cigars are delicious served with vanilla ice-cream for a light and easy dessert. Ripe bananas work best.

SERVES: 4

PREP TIME: 10 MINUTES

COOK TIME: 15–20 MINUTES

filo pastry 6 sheets
butter 50g, melted
ground cinnamon 1 teaspoon
brown sugar 2 teaspoons
pistachios 1 cup finely chopped + extra to serve
bananas 4 (try to choose bananas that are not too bent)
runny honey to serve
natural unsweetened thick Greek yoghurt to serve

Per serve
Energy: 1717kj (410 cal)
Carbohydrate: 43.2g
Protein: 8.1g
Fat: 26.8g
Saturated fat: 7.7g

1 Preheat oven to 180°C. Lay a sheet of filo on the bench and brush with melted butter, place a second layer on top, brush with melted butter and lay a final third layer of filo pastry on top. Cut in half so you have two large squares. Repeat with remaining sheets of filo, so you end up with four large squares of pastry (each 3 sheets thick). Brush the top layer of filo with melted butter, sprinkle over cinnamon and brown sugar and scatter over pistachios.

2 Place each banana, widthways, in the middle of each filo square. Bend banana to straighten it out a bit (it is fine if it breaks a little). Firmly roll pastry around banana, enclosing pistachios.

3 Place cigars on a baking tray with pastry seam underneath. Brush with melted butter and bake for 15–20 minutes until golden and crispy. To serve, drizzle over honey and scatter over more pistachios. Serve cigars hot with a dollop of Greek yoghurt.

Healthy Sorbets, Gelato *and* Ice-cream

Healthy and ice-cream don't normally go together in the same sentence, but these treats, with all the fruit, are good for you, too!

SERVES: 4

PREP TIME: 10–15 MINUTES

FREEZING TIME: 8 HOURS

Black Doris Plum Sorbet

Drain an 850g can of Black Doris plums, reserving the juice. Cut plums in half and remove stones. Place plums in a dish or container, or on a tray lined with baking paper, and freeze overnight until hard. Allow plums to thaw on the bench for 5–10 minutes if very hard (this makes it easier to blend). Place frozen plums in a food processor with a couple of tablespoons of reserved plum juice, and blend until smooth. Serve immediately or return to container and freeze until ready to serve.

Per serve
Energy: 644kj (152 cal)
Carbohydrate: 23.6g
Protein: 2.5g
Fat: 1.1g
Saturated fat: 0g

Kiwifruit *and* Honey Sorbet

Peel and slice 7–8 ripe green kiwifruit, and place in a dish or container, or on a tray lined with baking paper. Freeze overnight until hard. Allow kiwifruit to thaw on the bench for 5–10 minutes if very hard (this makes it easier to blend). Place frozen kiwifruit in a food processor with the juice of 1 lime, 2 tablespoons of runny honey and 1 egg white, and blitz until smooth. Return to container and freeze until firm and ready to serve.

Per serve
Energy: 495kj (117 cal)
Carbohydrate: 23.6g
Protein: 2.5g
Fat: 1.1g
Saturated fat: 0g

Banana Choc-chip Ice-cream

Peel and chop 5 bananas and place in a dish or container, or on a tray lined with baking paper. Freeze overnight until hard. Allow banana to thaw at room temperature for 10 minutes before blending (this makes it easier to blend). Place frozen bananas, ½ cup of cream and 3 tablespoons of icing sugar in a food processor and blitz until smooth, and the consistency of ice-cream. Transfer to a large mixing bowl and fold through 80g of good-quality dark eating chocolate, chopped. Serve immediately or return to freezer until ready to serve.

Per serve
Energy: 1727kj (407 cal)
Carbohydrate: 58.0g
Protein: 3.4g
Fat: 18.8g
Saturated fat: 11.4g

Mango, Avocado *and* Vanilla Gelato

Chop the flesh of 2 firm, ripe avocados and 2 large sweet mangoes and place in a dish or container, or on a tray lined with baking paper. Freeze overnight, until hard. Thaw avocados and mango for 10 minutes before blending (this makes it easier to blend). Place frozen avocado, frozen mango, 1 teaspoon of vanilla essence or extract, 3 tablespoons of icing sugar, 3–4 tablespoons of coconut cream and the juice of 1 lime in a food processor and blitz until smooth. Serve immediately or return to freezer until ready to serve.

Per serve
Energy: 1207kj (285 cal)
Carbohydrate: 21.5g
Protein: 2.0g
Fat: 21.9g
Saturated fat: 3.9g

Feijoa *and* Rhubarb Almond Crumble *with* Ginger *and* Brown Sugar Yoghurt

Rhubarb and feijoas go really well with a slight kick of warming ginger. And wait until you discover how delicious fresh grated ginger mixed with brown sugar and mascarpone is! The almonds give the crumble a sweet, crunchy nuttiness.

1 Combine feijoas, rhubarb and orange juice in a saucepan. Bring to the boil, then lower heat and simmer, uncovered, for 15–20 minutes, stirring frequently, until fruit collapses. Stir in honey.

2 To make the crumble, stir ground almonds, oats, ginger, cinnamon and brown sugar together. Rub in butter using your fingertips until mixture resembles breadcrumbs.

3 Preheat oven to 180°C. Spoon stewed fruit into a baking dish and sprinkle crumble mixture over the top. Bake for 15–20 minutes until crumble is golden brown.

4 Mix yoghurt or mascarpone, grated fresh ginger and brown sugar together. To serve, spoon some crumble into each bowl and top with a dollop of ginger and brown sugar yoghurt.

SERVES: 6

PREP TIME: 15 MINUTES

COOK TIME: 30–40 MINUTES

feijoas 600g, flesh scooped out
rhubarb stalks 400g, chopped
orange juice of 2
runny honey 3–4 tablespoons to taste

CRUMBLE TOPPING

blanched ground almonds 1½ cups
rolled oats 1 cup
ground ginger 1 teaspoon
ground cinnamon 1 teaspoon
brown sugar ¼ cup
butter 50g, softened

GINGER AND BROWN SUGAR YOGHURT

thick Greek yoghurt or mascarpone 1 cup
fresh ginger 1½ teaspoons finely grated
brown sugar 1 tablespoon

Per serve
Energy: 2108kj (503 cal)
Carbohydrate: 38.3g
Protein: 13.8g
Fat: 33.5g
Saturated fat: 8.6g

Sticky Red Wine Pears *with* Cinnamon Crème Fraîche

If you want to impress your dinner guests but want to do so with little effort, serve these sticky red wine pears. Place everything in the saucepan and let the pears infuse with the cinnamon and lemon while the red wine reduces to become a sweet, sticky syrup. Utterly delicious and so easy.

1 Cut a thin slice off the bottom of the pears so they will stand upright when served.

2 Place lemon peel, lemon juice, red wine, water, brown sugar, vanilla and cinnamon in a medium-sized saucepan and stir to combine. Add pears (don't worry if they fall on to their sides), cover and bring to the boil. As soon as syrup boils, reduce heat and simmer, uncovered, for 1 hour until pears are tender and a deep red colour. Baste pears with syrup a few times while cooking.

3 Carefully remove pears from syrup and set aside. Boil syrup for 5–10 minutes until it is a thick syrup.

4 Mix crème fraîche or Greek yoghurt with cinnamon. Serve pears with a dollop of cinnamon crème fraîche or yoghurt and a couple of tablespoons of syrup drizzled over the top.

Tip The pears will keep in the syrup in a covered container for a couple of weeks. The syrup can be reused to poach other fruit, or reduced down further to make a sticky dessert syrup to drizzle over ice-cream.

SERVES: 6

PREP TIME: 15 MINUTES

COOK TIME: 1 HOUR 15 MINUTES

STICKY RED WINE PEARS

pears 6 just ripe, peeled with stalks on
lemon smooth-skinned, peel of 1, cut into thin strips
lemon juice of 1 (use peeled lemon above)
red wine (e.g. pinot noir or syrah) 2 cups
water 1 cup
brown sugar 1 cup
vanilla pod scraped seeds of 1
cinnamon sticks 2

CINNAMON CRÈME FRAÎCHE

crème fraîche or **natural unsweetened thick Greek yoghurt** ⅔ cup
ground cinnamon ¼ teaspoon

DAIRY FREE GLUTEN FREE

(Dairy free without crème fraîche)

Per serve
Energy: 1039kj (248 cal)
Carbohydrate: 43.1g
Protein: 0.6g
Fat: 0.5g
Saturated fat: 0.0g

Grilled Peaches *with* Berry Sauce *and* Pistachio Crumble Topping

This dessert is great to serve at a dinner party — it's light enough to end a meal without your guests feeling overly full, but with the clever crumble topping it still counts as pudding. What's great is you can make all the components — roasted peaches, berry sauce, crumble — in advance, simply heat in the oven and assemble when ready to serve.

1 Preheat oven grill to high. Place peaches cut side up in an ovenproof dish. Sieve icing sugar over peaches. Grill for 15 minutes until soft and slightly caramelised on top. When the peaches are ready, remove from oven and set aside to cool a little (they will be very, very hot). Change oven setting to bake at 180°C.

2 Meanwhile, make the berry sauce and crumble topping. Place berries in a small saucepan with icing sugar and a splash of water. Bring to the boil and cook for about 5 minutes, stirring frequently, until reduced to a sauce. Set aside.

3 To make the crumble, combine oats, cinnamon and brown sugar in a bowl. Rub in butter with your fingertips until mixture resembles breadcrumbs. Mix in pistachio nuts. Spread crumble mixture over a baking tray and bake for 10–12 minutes until golden brown.

4 To serve, divide berry sauce between bowls, and place two grilled peach halves on top. Sprinkle over pistachio crumble and serve with a dollop of Greek yoghurt or crème fraîche on the side.

SERVES: 4

PREP TIME: 5 MINUTES

COOK TIME: 25 MINUTES

GRILLED PEACHES

peaches 4 large ripe, halved and stoned
icing sugar 1 tablespoon

BERRY SAUCE

boysenberries or **raspberries** fresh or frozen, 2 cups (250g)
icing sugar 2 tablespoons

PISTACHIO CRUMBLE

rolled oats ½ cup
cinnamon ¼ teaspoon
brown sugar 1 tablespoon
butter 25g, softened
pistachio nuts ⅓ cup, finely chopped
natural unsweetened Greek yoghurt or **crème fraîche** to serve

Per serve
Energy: 1311kj (313 cal)
Carbohydrate: 32.4g
Protein: 8.5g
Fat: 16.9g
Saturated fat: 7.6g

Melon, Honey *and* Coconut Sago Pudding

People seem to either love or hate the gelatinous texture of sago. I love this creamy, sweet pudding which I grew up with living in Malaysia. If you pour the sago into little moulds it will set in the fridge, which you can then unmould and serve cold with a little more coconut drizzled on top.

1 Combine sago or tapioca and water in a medium-sized saucepan. Bring to the boil while stirring. Reduce heat and simmer for 7–8 minutes, stirring occasionally, or until sago is cooked. It is cooked when most of the white balls have turned clear and the sago is thick and gluggy.

2 Mix in honey to taste, coconut milk, milk and diced fresh fruit. Serve immediately with more honey drizzled on top if desired.

SERVES: 4–5

PREP TIME: 5 MINUTES

COOK TIME: 10 MINUTES

sago or **tapioca pearls** ²/₃ cup
water 1½ cups
honey 2–3 tablespoons to taste
coconut milk ¼ cup
milk ¼ cup
rock melon and/or **honeydew** and/or **mango** 1½ cups diced

DAIRY FREE   GLUTEN FREE

(Dairy free with extra coconut milk instead)

Per serve
Energy: 541kj (122 cal)
Carbohydrate: 30.5g
Protein: 1.3g
Fat: 0.3g
Saturated fat: 0.1g

Grilled Stone Fruit *with* Red Wine Syrup

This makes a simple yet elegant dessert. Serve individually or on a large platter placed in the centre of the table so everyone can help themselves.

1 Place red wine, lemon peel and juice, brown sugar, vanilla and cinnamon in a medium-sized saucepan and boil down until thick and syrupy, 10–15 minutes. The amount of liquid should reduce by more than half.

2 Preheat oven grill to high. Arrange apricots, plums and nectarines or peaches, cut side up, in a baking dish. Sieve icing sugar all over fruit. Grill fruit for 12–15 minutes until soft and caramelised on top. Watch that it doesn't burn.

3 Arrange grilled fruit on a platter, add cherries and drizzle over red wine syrup. Serve with a bowl of Greek yoghurt, mascarpone or ice-cream on the side, for everyone to help themselves.

SERVES: 4

PREP TIME: 10 MINUTES

COOK TIME: 15 MINUTES

RED WINE SYRUP

red wine (e.g. pinot noir) 2 cups
lemon smooth-skinned peel of 1, cut into thin strips (avoid white pith)
lemon juice of 1 (use peeled lemon above)
brown sugar 1 cup
vanilla pod scraped seeds of 1
cinnamon stick 1

GRILLED STONE FRUIT

apricots 4 just ripe, halved
plums 4 just ripe, halved
nectarines or **peaches** 2 ripe, halved
icing sugar 2–3 tablespoons
cherries 12
natural unsweetened Greek yoghurt, **ice-cream** or **mascarpone** to serve

(Dairy free without yoghurt, ice-cream or mascarpone)

Per serve
Energy: 1815kj (433 cal)
Carbohydrate: 61.7g
Protein: 5.2g
Fat: 7.0g
Saturated fat: 3.8g

Creamy Mango Ice-blocks

I have fond memories of making all sorts of different flavoured ice-blocks when I was a kid. My mother didn't mind us making and eating them, as most of the time it was just puréed fruit. And we thought we were getting a treat!

1 Blend all ingredients together in a blender or food processor until smooth.

2 Pour into ice-block moulds and freeze until hard.

MAKES: 6–8 ICE-BLOCKS

PREP TIME: 5–10 MINUTES

mangoes 2 large ripe, peeled and chopped
thick coconut cream ¾ cup
natural sweetened yoghurt ¼ cup
vanilla extract or **essence** 1 teaspoon
runny honey 2–3 tablespoons to taste

(Dairy free with extra coconut cream instead of yoghurt)

Per serve
Energy: 341kj (81 cal)
Carbohydrate: 13.1g
Protein: 0.5g
Fat: 3.1g
Saturated fat: 2.7g

Cherries *with* Chocolate *and* Red Wine Syrup

This easy dessert is one to share around the table, with a big bowl of fresh cherries in the middle making a stunning centrepiece. Serve the syrup in a bowl on the side for everyone to dip their cherries into.

SERVES: 4–6

PREP TIME: 5 MINUTES

COOK TIME: 5–10 MINUTES

dark eating chocolate good-quality, 100g, broken into pieces
red wine (e.g. pinot noir or syrah) 1½ cups
brown sugar 3 tablespoons
cinnamon stick 1, broken
star anise 2
cherries fresh ripe 1kg

GLUTEN FREE

Per serve
Energy: 1313kj (313 cal)
Carbohydrate: 45.7g
Protein: 3.1g
Fat: 6.7g
Saturated fat: 3.5g

1 Combine chocolate, red wine, brown sugar, cinnamon and star anise in a small saucepan. Bring to the boil, stirring constantly with a wooden spoon. Simmer for 5 minutes, stirring frequently, until the chocolate has melted and the syrup is thick and smooth.

2 Serve syrup in a bowl and dip in cherries.

Coconut Vanilla Yoghurt Panna Cotta *with* Marinated Berries

This is my much lighter yet still delicious version of the classic dessert, with beautiful flavours of vanilla and coconut. Panna cotta is a great dessert to make for a dinner party because it can be prepared up to a few days in advance and looks stunning when plated up. The berries can be marinated in other fruit liqueurs — try framboise (strawberry), for example.

SERVES: 6

PREP TIME: 15 MINUTES

SETTING TIME: 4 HOURS

VANILLA YOGHURT PANNA COTTA

- **gelatine leaves*** 3½
- **coconut cream** 1⅓ cups
- **vanilla-flavoured** or **natural sweetened yoghurt** 1⅔ cups
- **vanilla extract** or **essence** ½ teaspoon (or 1 teaspoon if using natural yoghurt)
- **boiling water** 3 tablespoons
- **honey** 3–4 tablespoons to taste
- **coconut oil** or **neutral oil** (e.g. canola, soy or rice bran) or **butter** for greasing

MARINATED BERRIES

- **berries** fresh or frozen, 2 cups
- **cassis** (blackcurrant liqueur) ½ cup

GLUTEN FREE

Per serve
Energy: 1044kj (249 cal)
Carbohydrate: 14.2g
Protein: 5.2g
Fat: 12.6g
Saturated fat: 10.1g

1 Soak gelatine leaves in cold water for 5–10 minutes.

2 Whisk coconut cream, yoghurt and vanilla together.

3 Remove soaked gelatine leaves from cold water and dissolve in boiling water. Add honey and stir until dissolved. Whisk gelatine and honey mixture into yoghurt mixture until well combined. Transfer mixture into a pouring jug (for easier pouring).

4 Lightly grease six dariole moulds or small teacups or ramekins with oil or butter. Pour mixture into moulds, dividing equally. Refrigerate until set (at least 4 hours or overnight).

5 Place berries in a bowl and pour over cassis. Leave to marinate for at least 30 minutes, or until ready to serve.

6 To serve, briefly dip moulds into hot water for 5–10 seconds and run the blunt edge of a knife around the inside of the mould to loosen. Carefully tip out onto a plate. Repeat with remaining panna cotta. Just before serving, spoon over some marinated berries and cassis.

*Tip Alternatively, you can use 3½ teaspoons gelatine powder mixed with 3 tablespoons cold water. Leave to swell, then dissolve in 2–3 tablespoons boiling water.

Chilled Lemon Soufflés

These light and airy soufflés are really more like a chilled lemon mousse. The appearance of a soufflé that has 'risen' is cleverly created by a paper collar put around the dish before it is filled with the mousse. Once the mousse has set, you remove the paper collars to reveal soufflés that will never flop!

SERVES: 6

PREP TIME: 25 MINUTES

SETTING TIME: 4 HOURS

gelatine leaves* 2½
eggs 6, separated
lemon juice ½ cup
lemons finely grated zest of 2
caster sugar ½ cup
boiling water 2 tablespoons
caster sugar ¾ cup
cream or **natural unsweetened thick
   Greek yoghurt** 1 cup

GLUTEN
FREE

Per serve
Energy: 1676kj (400 cal)
Carbohydrate: 46.3g
Protein: 8.3g
Fat: 20.8g
Saturated fat: 11.4g

1 Wrap the *outside* of 6 medium ramekins with a thick strip of baking paper, so there is an 8cm collar above the ramekins (this will help support the soufflé as it sets). Secure baking paper in place firmly with cellotape or string.

2 Soak gelatine leaves in cold water for 5–10 minutes.

3 Meanwhile, make a lemon curd. Whisk egg yolks, lemon juice and zest and first measure of caster sugar together in the top of a double boiler or a glass bowl. Set over a saucepan of simmering water. Whisk mixture continuously until it thickens enough to coat the back of a wooden spoon, 8–10 minutes.

4 Remove gelatine from cold water and dissolve in boiling water. Whisk dissolved gelatine mixture into still-hot lemon curd. Set aside to cool slightly.

5 Use an electric beater to beat egg whites until soft peaks form. Add second measure of caster sugar and continue beating on high until thick and glossy, 3–4 minutes.

6 Whip cream to soft peaks. Use a large metal spoon to gently fold all three mixtures together until just combined. Spoon mixture into ramekins, coming 4–5cm above ramekins, and refrigerate until set (at least 4 hours or overnight). To serve, remove baking paper collar from ramekins. Behold — you have a tall soufflé that won't flop! Serve with a dollop of whipped cream or yoghurt on the side.

*Tip Alternatively, use 2½ teaspoons gelatine powder soaked in 3 tablespoons cold water. Leave to swell, then dissolve in 2–3 tablespoons of boiling water.

treats & home baking

It's healthy to treat yourself once in a while — having a relaxed attitude towards food is an important part of a sustainable and enjoyable way of eating. It's all about moderation and watching portion sizes — eat half a cake and you will gain weight, a thin slice and you'll be satisfied, and won't gain an ounce.

In this section you'll find foods that fit more into the 'once in a while' category — mouth-watering cakes for special occasions that taste just as impressive as they look. It's in my nature to always try to make things healthier, so many of these recipes are lower in saturated fat and sugar and higher in fibre (with sneaky added vegetables) than their usual counterparts. That said, I would still never deem them healthy enough to be eaten as anything more than a treat.

There are also a couple of home-made bread recipes as I think it's great if you can make your own, avoiding the often preservative-laden bread that is commonly sold in supermarkets.

You needn't worry about breaking the healthy eating 'rules' every now and again, because it's how you eat most of the time that matters, not the occasional indulgence. Remember, that can do lots of good for us, too! As a rule of thumb, eat well 90 per cent of the time, and for the other 10 per cent feel free to have a little of whatever takes your fancy. And when you do, make sure you enjoy it.

Lime *and* Coconut Macaroons

Not to be confused with French macaroons, these little fluffy coconut meringue delights are gluten free and dairy free. They keep well in an airtight container and are nice to have with a cup of coffee. Or serve them with fruit, ice-cream and a drizzle of passionfruit syrup for dessert (see page 253).

MAKES: 18

PREP TIME: 10 MINUTES

COOK TIME: 30 MINUTES

egg whites* 3
caster sugar ¾ cup
white vinegar ¼ teaspoon
blanched ground almonds ½ cup
thread coconut** 2 cups
limes finely grated zest of 3

Per serve
Energy: 575kj (137 cal)
Carbohydrate: 11.8g
Protein: 2.1g
Fat: 9.2g
Saturated fat: 6.1g

1 Preheat oven to 150°C (do not use fanbake). Line a baking tray with baking paper. Place egg whites in a large clean mixing bowl and beat with an electric beater until soft peaks form. Gradually add sugar in a steady stream while beating continuously. Add vinegar and continue beating on high speed for 5 minutes until mixture is thick and glossy.

2 Fold through ground almonds, coconut and lime zest.

3 Drop heaped tablespoons of mixture onto lined baking tray. Bake in preheated oven for 30 minutes.

4 Remove and allow to cool completely before storing. Serve as is, or with passionfruit syrup (see page 253) drizzled over top just before serving.

*Tip For best results, use eggs that are at least 1 week old and at room temperature. The whites of older eggs beat up much better than very fresh eggs.

**Tip Thread coconut, sometimes also called shredded coconut, is different to desiccated coconut — it comes in much longer, thicker strands.

Mocha Hazelnut Layer Cake

This is an indulgent moist dessert cake with coffee, chocolate, Irish cream liqueur and hazelnuts, not dissimilar to a tiramisu. If you don't want to use alcohol, substitute a mix of condensed and evaporated milk instead. If you would prefer to make your own chocolate sponge cakes, follow the sponge cake recipe on page 247, adding ¼ cup of good-quality dark cocoa powder to the flours.

SERVES: 8–10

PREP TIME: 15–20 MINUTES

CHILLING TIME: 2 HOURS

raisins 1 cup
very strong coffee ¾ cup (espresso is preferable, but plunger or filter is fine)
Irish cream liqueur ¾ cup
dark eating chocolate good-quality, 175g, chopped
crème fraîche or **mascarpone** 250g
chocolate sponge cakes 2 round roughly 20cm (storebought or see page 247)
hazelnuts ⅓ cup chopped
finely ground coffee 1 tablespoon (optional)

Per serve
Energy: 2998kj (716 cal)
Carbohydrate: 94.2g
Protein: 11.4g
Fat: 31.2g
Saturated fat: 18.2g

1. Pour boiling water over raisins to cover and leave to soak and plump up. Drain raisins once cool. Mix coffee with liqueur.

2. Melt chocolate in a double boiler or a glass bowl set over a saucepan of simmering water, making sure the base of the bowl doesn't touch the water. Beat crème fraîche or mascarpone to soften and add to melted chocolate. Stir together until smooth.

3. Place one chocolate sponge on a plate. Brush half of the coffee liqueur mixture evenly over sponge (it will be quite wet). Spread over half the chocolate mixture with a spatula (see tip below). Scatter over the raisins. Place the second sponge cake on top. Gently but firmly push down so that the two cakes sandwich together. Brush top cake with remaining coffee liqueur mixture. Spread remaining chocolate mixture over the top of the cake and on the sides using a butter or palette knife. Sprinkle over hazelnuts.

4. Refrigerate for at least 2 hours or up to 2 days until ready to serve.

5. Sieve ground coffee if using over cake and stand at room temperature for 30 minutes before serving.

Tip Warm chocolate mixture for 5–10 seconds in microwave to loosen if necessary. Dip your knife into hot water, then dry it, a few times while icing — this will make it easier to spread the icing.

Wholemeal Kumara Bread

This is my husband's bread recipe. There are no preservatives, unlike commercially made breads, so is best enjoyed within a day or two of baking. Alternatively, slice and freeze the bread to avoid it going stale. I've given you the option of using caraway or cumin seeds, which have very different flavours but are equally nice in the bread.

1   Cook kumara in boiling salted water until soft, 10–15 minutes. Drain and mash well with a little salt to taste.

2   While kumara is cooking, combine yeast, sugar and warm water in a bowl. Leave on the bench until frothy, 5–10 minutes.

3   In a large mixing bowl, combine flours, salt, thyme or rosemary and caraway or cumin seeds. Add oil, kumara mash and yeast mixture and mix until well combined.

4   Knead dough on a lightly floured surface, adding a little extra flour as necessary, until dough is soft and elastic, about 10 minutes.

5   Place dough in a lightly oiled bowl and cover with cling film. Leave to rise in a warm place for 25 minutes.

6   Line a baking tray with baking paper. Cut dough in half and shape into two loaves. Place loaves on prepared baking tray and leave to rise for a further 20 minutes.

7   When ready to bake bread, preheat oven to 200°C. Place ½ cup boiling water in a small ovenproof dish in the oven to create steam (this helps to create a nice crust on the bread).

8   Cut 1cm thick slashes across dough with a sharp paring knife and dust with a little flour. Bake for 25 minutes or until a crust has developed and the base sounds firm and hollow when tapped. Remove from oven and allow to cool on a rack.

MAKES: 2 LOAVES

PREP TIME: 20 MINUTES

RISING TIME: 45 MINUTES

COOK TIME: 25 MINUTES

orange kumara 300g (approx. 1 medium), peeled and chopped
active dried yeast 1 tablespoon
sugar 1 teaspoon
lukewarm water 1 cup
high-grade flour 1 cup + extra for kneading and dusting
wholemeal flour 2 cups
salt 1½ teaspoons
fresh thyme or **rosemary** 2 tablespoons, finely chopped
caraway or **cumin seeds** 1 tablespoon
extra virgin olive oil 2 tablespoons

DAIRY FREE   VEG

Per serve
Energy: 269 kj (64 cal)
Carbohydrate: 10.8g
Protein: 2.0g
Fat: 1.4g
Saturated fat: 0.2g

Sundried Tomato, Herb *and* Parmesan Pizza Bread

Nothing beats the aroma or taste of freshly baked pizza bread straight out of the oven. This is ideal as a casual appetiser to a meal.

MAKES: 4 PIZZA BREADS

PREP TIME: 20 MINUTES

RISING TIME: 30–45 MINUTES

COOK TIME: 12–15 MINUTES

active dried yeast 2 teaspoons
sugar 1½ teaspoons
lukewarm water 1 cup
high-grade flour 2 cups
semolina ¾ cup
salt 1½ teaspoons
fresh oregano, **rosemary** or **thyme**
   2 tablespoons chopped + extra for
   sprinkling
sundried tomatoes ½ cup sliced
garlic 2 cloves, minced
extra virgin olive oil 2 tablespoons +
   extra for drizzling.
parmesan cheese ¼ cup grated

(VEG)

Per serve
Energy: 940 kj (225 cal)
Carbohydrate: 35.7g
Protein: 7.4g
Fat: 5.9g
Saturated fat: 1.1g

1 Combine yeast, sugar and lukewarm water in a bowl. Set aside on the bench until frothy, about 10 minutes. Stir together well.

2 Mix flour, semolina, salt, herbs, sundried tomatoes and garlic together. Add to yeast mixture, along with extra virgin olive oil. Mix together until well combined. You may need to add a tablespoon more of water to get it all to stick together.

3 Knead dough on a lightly floured surface until smooth and elastic. This will take about 10 minutes. Place dough in a lightly oiled bowl, cover with cling film, and leave to prove in a warm place for 30–45 minutes until double in size.

4 When ready to cook, preheat oven to 220°C. Preheat a pizza stone or oven tray lined with baking paper.

5 Cut dough into four, and roll out each piece to about 5mm thick. Sprinkle with parmesan cheese and more herbs and place on preheated pizza stone or tray. Bake for 12–15 minutes until parmesan is melted and bread is slightly puffed and cooked through. Drizzle with extra virgin olive oil, cut into pieces and serve immediately.

Butternut Cupcakes *with* Cream Cheese Icing *and* Beetroot Sugar

The taste of these gluten-free butternut cupcakes reminds me of carrot cake. They are quite moist cupcakes and un-iced they freeze well. The pink beetroot sugar is so clever — no artificial colour needed here!

1 Preheat oven to 190°C (170°C fanbake). Lightly grease and line a medium 12-hole muffin pan with paper cases. Mix all muffin ingredients together in a large mixing bowl until well combined. (You don't have to worry about over-mixing the muffin batter as there is no gluten in it.)

2 Spoon mixture into paper cases, filling to the top. Bake for 30–35 minutes or until a skewer inserted in the centre of the muffins comes out clean. Stand for a few minutes before turning out to cool on a wire rack. Leave to cool completely before icing.

3 To make icing, beat cream cheese with icing sugar and lemon juice until smooth.

4 To make the betroot sugar, bash grated beetroot with a teaspoon of sugar in a mortar and pestle until a paste forms, then stir in the rest of the sugar. To assemble, spread icing over cupcakes and sprinkle over beetroot sugar.

*Tip Peel 700g butternut and chop into 2.5cm cubes. Roast at 180°C for 30 minutes or until soft, then mash.

MAKES: 12 CUPCAKES

PREP TIME: 15 MINUTES + 30 MINUTES TO ROAST BUTTERNUT

COOK TIME: 30–35 MINUTES

CUPCAKES

golden syrup ¼ cup or **brown sugar** ½ cup
vanilla extract or **essence** 1 teaspoon
oil (e.g. canola, soy or rice bran) ¼ cup
eggs 3, beaten
mixed spice 1 teaspoon
blanched ground almonds 2 cups
desiccated coconut ½ cup
baking powder 2 teaspoons
mashed roasted butternut* 2 cups
lemon or **orange** finely grated zest of 1

CREAM CHEESE ICING

cream cheese 150g, softened
icing sugar ¼ cup
lemon juice 1–2 tablespoons

BEETROOT SUGAR

grated beetroot 1 teaspoon
sugar ¼ cup

(Check baking powder is gluten free)

Per serve
Energy: 1431kj (341 cal)
Carbohydrate: 28.5g
Protein: 7.9g
Fat: 23.5g
Saturated fat: 5.8g

Little Maple
Walnut Cookies

These cute little gluten-free cookies were inspired by my favourite ice-cream flavour — maple walnut!

MAKES: 22–24 LITTLE COOKIES

PREP TIME: 10–15 MINUTES

COOK TIME: 18–20 MINUTES

blanched ground almonds 2 cups
shredded or **desiccated coconut** ½ cup
ground cinnamon 1 teaspoon
butter 50g, melted
maple syrup ½ cup
milk 4 tablespoons
walnut halves 24

(Dairy free with coconut or soy milk)

Per serve
Energy: 478 kj (114 cal)
Carbohydrate: 6.7g
Protein: 3.1g
Fat: 9.2g
Saturated fat: 2.5g

1 Preheat oven to 170°C (150°C fanbake). Line a baking tray with baking paper. In a large mixing bowl, mix all ingredients except walnuts together until well combined.

2 Roll tablespoonsful of mixture into balls and place on prepared baking tray. Flatten slightly with the back of a wet teaspoon and push a walnut half in.

3 Bake for 18–20 minutes until light golden.

4 Remove and allow to cool completely on a wire rack. These cookies will keep for up to a week in an airtight container.

Dark Chocolate, Date *and* Beetroot Cake

This is a very moist, almost fudgey chocolate cake. The intense dark chocolate, earthy beetroot and caramel notes from the dates result in a richly flavoured cake that is not overly sweet. Use the best-quality dark chocolate and cocoa you can afford.

1 Preheat oven to 200°C (180°C fanbake). Wrap whole beetroot in tinfoil and bake for 45 minutes or until a skewer easily goes through the middle. Unwrap beetroot and cool before scraping off skin. Roughly chop.

2 Lower oven temperature to 180°C. Grease and line a 21–23cm round springform cake tin with baking paper.

3 Place dates and water in a small saucepan. Boil for 5 minutes, stirring frequently, until dates are mashed up.

4 Pureé beetroot with yoghurt in a food processor or blender until well combined. Add eggs, sugar and mashed dates, and blitz until well combined.

5 Melt chocolate gently in a double boiler or a glass bowl set over a saucepan of simmering water, making sure the bowl does not touch the water. Stir in oil.

6 In a large mixing bowl, combine ground almonds, flour, cocoa powder and baking powder. Add melted chocolate and beetroot mixtures and use a large metal spoon to fold together. Do not over-mix.

7 Pour mixture into prepared cake tin and bake for 60 minutes until cake springs back when lightly pressed. The cake is quite fudgey so a skewer inserted into the middle will not come out clean. Stand 5–10 minutes before removing from tin. When cake has cooled, ice with chocolate icing.

8 To make the icing, melt chocolate gently in a double boiler or a glass bowl over simmering water. Stir in oil. Ice cooled cake and serve with Greek yoghurt, ice-cream or whipped cream.

SERVES: 10–12

PREP TIME: 20 MINUTES + 45 MINUTES TO PRE-COOK BEETROOT

COOK TIME: 1 HOUR

beetroot 250g (about 1 medium)
dates 2 cups, chopped (about 300–350g)
water ¾ cup
natural unsweetened thick Greek yoghurt ¾ cup
eggs 4
sugar ¾ cup
dark eating chocolate (60–72% cocoa) good-quality, 150g, broken into pieces
nut or **neutral oil** (e.g. canola, soy or rice bran) ¾ cup
blanched ground almonds 1 cup
plain flour 1 cup
cocoa powder good-quality, ¼ cup
baking powder 1 teaspoon

ICING

dark eating chocolate good quality, 100g, broken into pieces
nut or **neutral oil** (eg. canola, soy or rice bran) 1 teaspoon

TO SERVE

natural unsweetened thick Greek yoghurt, **ice-cream** or **cream**

Per serve
Energy: 2468kj (590 cal)
Carbohydrate: 52.5g
Protein: 11.1g
Fat: 37.9g
Saturated fat: 7.5g

Turkish Rose Pavlova

This dessert is a show-stopper. It's so easy to make, yet looks a million bucks. This is my no-fail pavlova recipe that results in a crisp shell and marshmallowy centre every time. It's key you leave the pavlova to cool in the oven completely without opening the door. Once cooked, it will keep in an airtight container for a few days.

1 Preheat oven to 130°C (do not use fan-bake). Line a baking tray with baking paper and draw a 20cm circle on it using a plate as a stencil.

2 Place egg whites in a clean, dry bowl and beat with an electric beater until stiff peaks form. Gradually add caster sugar while continuously beating. Continue beating on high speed for 10 minutes until all the sugar has dissolved and meringue mixture is thick and glossy. Beat in cornflour and vinegar.

3 Spoon meringue mixture into the circle on the baking paper, making sure the circle is fully covered. If you like you can smooth the top of the mixture out to create a flat surface, but I prefer to leave it in dollops and swirls.

4 Bake in oven for 1 hour 15 minutes. Turn off oven and leave to completely cool in oven without opening oven door. Once cooled, the pavlova can be stored in a large, dry, airtight container for a few days.

5 When ready to serve pavlova, whip cream, icing sugar, vanilla and rose water if using until soft peaks form. Dollop cream over pavlova and decorate with Turkish delight, strawberries, pistachios and rose petals if using.

*Tip For best results, make sure the eggs are at room temperature and ideally at least a week old as they whip up much better than very fresh eggs.

SERVES: 8

PREP TIME: 15–20 MINUTES

COOK TIME: 1 HOUR 15 MINUTES

PAVLOVA

egg whites* 7
caster sugar 1½ cups
cornflour 2 teaspoons
white vinegar 1 teaspoon

TOPPING

cream 1 cup
icing sugar ¼ cup
vanilla pod scraped seeds of 1
rose water 1 teaspoon (optional)
Turkish delight pink (rose-flavoured), 200g chopped
strawberries ½ punnet, sliced
pistachios ¼ cup shelled, roughly chopped
pink rose petals to garnish (optional)

GLUTEN FREE

Per serve
Energy: 1531 kj (366 cal)
Carbohydrate: 70.6g
Protein: 4.1g
Fat: 15.0g
Saturated fat: 8.0g

Passionfruit, Lime, Banana *and* Coconut Sponge

Sweet and tangy passionfruit and lime curd sandwiched between sponge cake with cream and coconut makes a fabulous cake for a special occasion.

SERVES: 8

PREP TIME: 35–40 MINUTES

COOK TIME: 20 MINUTES

SPONGE CAKES

- **melted butter** for greasing
- **cornflour** 2 teaspoons for dusting
- **eggs** 3, separated
- **caster sugar** ¾ cup
- **vanilla extract** or **essence** 1 teaspoon
- **cornflour** ½ cup
- **plain flour** ¼ cup
- **baking powder** 1 teaspoon
- **golden syrup** 2 teaspoons, dissolved in
- **boiling water** 1 tablespoon

LIME PASSIONFRUIT CURD

- **egg yolks** 4
- **lime juice** ¼ cup
- **limes** finely grated zest of 3
- **caster sugar** ⅓ cup
- **passionfruit pulp** ¼ cup

FILLING AND TOPPING

- **cream cheese** 150g, softened
- **cream** 1 cup
- **bananas** 2 ripe, sliced

TO GARNISH

- **passionfruit pulp** 2–3 tablespoons
- **toasted thread coconut** ¼ cup

Per serve
Energy: 1695 kj (405 cal)
Carbohydrate: 41.3g
Protein: 5.7g
Fat: 24.5g
Saturated fat: 14.3g

1 Preheat oven to 190°C (170°C fanbake). Brush 2 x 20cm cake or sponge tins with melted butter. Sprinkle over cornflour and shake to coat. This helps the sponge cake 'climb' the sides of the tin. Line the base of each tin with baking paper.

2 Place egg whites in a clean, dry bowl and beat with an electric beater until stiff peaks form. Beat in sugar, vanilla and first lot of egg yolks until all the sugar has dissolved.

3 Sift cornflour, flour and baking powder into egg mixture. Mix golden syrup with boiling water and add. Gently fold everything together using a large metal spoon.

4 Pour batter into prepared cake tins, dividing equally, and bake for 20 minutes until they spring back when lightly touched. Leave in tin for 5 minutes before turning out onto a wire rack.

5 Meanwhile, make lime and passionfruit curd. Whisk egg yolks, lime juice, lime zest, caster sugar and passionfruit pulp together in a double boiler or a glass bowl set over a saucepan of simmering water. Whisk mixture continuously until it thickens enough to coat the back of a wooden spoon, 8–10 minutes. Chill for at least 10 minutes.

6 Beat cream cheese and cooled curd with an electric beater until smooth. In another bowl, whip cream until soft peaks form, then fold into cream cheese mixture. Chill until ready to assemble cake.

7 Place one sponge on a serving plate or cake stand. Evenly spread half the cream mixture over sponge, going right to the edges. Top with banana slices and second sponge. Spread remaining cream mixture on top, dress with passionfruit pulp and sprinkle with toasted coconut.

essentials

Ingredient Tips

Red meat

You will get much better results with your meat if it is brought up to room temperature before cooking. Do not cook it straight from the fridge — if cooked to medium or less it will still be cold in the middle. And even if you like it well done, by the time it's cooked in the middle it will be overcooked on the outside.

To test for doneness, lightly touch the tip of your thumb to your first (index) finger; the muscle at the base of your thumb will feel soft and 'squidgy', similar to rare meat. Touching your thumb to your second (middle) finger will tighten this muscle slightly, making it firmer, like medium-rare meat. Touching your third (ring) finger indicates medium cooked, and touching your last little pinky finger indicates well done!

Resting meat is as important as the cooking process, as it allows the meat to reabsorb all those delicious juices. As a general rule, rest meat for 5–10 minutes for smaller cuts like steak, or 20 minutes for a larger cut like a roast. Covering the meat with tinfoil and tea towels will prevent it from going cold while resting.

Chicken

For best results, chicken should not be cooked straight from the fridge; however, for food-safety reasons avoid leaving it out at room temperature for any more than an hour. Just like red meat, you should let chicken rest after it is cooked. Overcooked chicken can become dry, so try to avoid it — it is cooked when you insert the tip of a sharp knife into the deepest section of the chicken and the juices run clear, not pink.

Pork

Ethics aside, free-range pork tastes so much better than conventionally farmed pork. So for the pigs' welfare (and your tastebuds!) I highly recommend only ever buying free-range pork. You will get a more succulent and tasty result. Like chicken, avoid overcooking pork as it can dry out easily.

Duck

Asian restaurants and food stores sell beautifully roasted duck, which is handy for making instantly delicious soups and salads. If cooking duck yourself, score the skin with a sharp knife to allow the fat to render out. Duck breasts should be cooked to medium, leaving the flesh a slight rosy-pink colour, unlike chicken. Ensure you rest it after cooking, just like any other meat.

Fish

To avoid using lots of oil to stop your fish sticking to the frypan, use a non-stick pan. Dusting the fish in flour before frying also helps. To get crispy skin on your fish, pan-fry skin side down first for 2–3 minutes, and push down with a fish slice to flatten the fillet so that all the skin makes contact with the pan. Then flip the fish over and cook for 1 more minute until just cooked through. You may need to cook it a bit more or less depending on the thickness of the fillets.

Eggs

Both fresh and older eggs have a place, depending on what you are using them for. For poached eggs, the fresher the better as the white will stay firm around the yolk. However, for beating egg whites for meringue, pavlova or macaroons, older eggs at room temperature are best as their whites are 'drier' and whip up better.

Fruit

Buy and eat fruit that is in season. It will be fresher and therefore tastier because it is picked and delivered at ripeness, with no long cold-storage periods required. (Some of the out-of-season fruit you find in supermarkets all year round has been in cold storage for several months!) In-season fruit and vegetables also have less degradation of nutrients, it's cheaper and you are supporting local New Zealand growers.

Rice

If you don't have a rice cooker, follow this method for perfectly cooked rice every time. Use a ratio of 2 parts rice to 3 parts water. Combine in a saucepan with a pinch of salt and bring to the boil. As soon as the water has come to the boil, reduce to lowest heat and cover the pan with a tight-fitting lid and cook on very low heat for 15 minutes. Turn off the heat and leave the rice, still covered, to steam for a further 8 minutes. Do not lift the lid during any time of the cooking or steaming process to avoid steam escaping. If your pan doesn't have a tight-fitting lid, cover the pan with tinfoil before placing the lid on top — this will keep the steam in.

You can add slices of ginger, garlic, kaffir lime leaves, lemon, cardamon and saffron to your rice for subtle hints of flavour.

Nuts and coconut

Once shelled, nuts go rancid (when the fat oxidates and goes off) after a few months. Always check them before using, and if they taste rancid, throw them out. (As well as tasting awful, rancid fats are not good for you!) Storing nuts in the fridge and freezer prolong their life.

When toasting any kind of nut the key is to keep moving them around in the pan and to watch them carefully — because of their high fat content they can burn very quickly! Toast pine nuts, shaved or slivered almonds and coconut in a dry frypan on medium heat for 1–2 minutes, tossing and moving around the pan frequently, until light golden. For larger nuts like hazelnuts, whole almonds and macadamias you can also toast them in a pan (they will just take longer), or roast them at 180°C for 10–15 minutes.

Baking

Taking the time to grease and line muffin and cake tins with baking paper will pay off — the last thing you want is them to stick to the tins after all your hard work! Use the base of the cake tin as a stencil and draw around it with a pencil on to the baking paper. Then cut the baking paper out with scissors for the perfect fit.

Folding refers to the technique of combining two mixtures together in a large 'scooping' motion. Use a large, wide metal spoon or rubber spatula to make deep scoops into the mixture, then lift mixture from the bottom up and 'fold' over to gently combine the ingredients together. Do not stir. This keeps the mixture light and airy (because it avoids popping too many air bubbles) for a better baking result.

Flavour Boosters

Lime and Sesame Dressing

Combine 1 tablespoon fish sauce or soy sauce, ¼ cup lime juice, 2 teaspoons brown sugar, 2 teaspoons sesame oil and 1 tablespoon neutral oil or nut oil (e.g. peanut, canola, rice bran or soy). Makes around ½ cup. Keeps in the fridge for weeks.

Ponzu Dressing

Ponzu is a delicious and refreshing Japanese dressing that combines soy sauce and citrus.

Combine ⅓ cup lime or lemon juice, ⅓ cup soy sauce, 2 tablespoons rice vinegar, 1 teaspoon sesame oil, 2 teaspoons sugar or mirin, and 1 tablespoon neutral oil (e.g. canola, soy or rice bran). Makes about 1 cup. Keeps in the fridge for weeks.

Red Wine Vinegar Dressing

Combine 3 tablespoons red wine vinegar, juice of ½ lemon, 3 tablespoons extra virgin olive oil, 2 teaspoons runny honey and 1 teaspoon wholegrain mustard. Makes about ½ cup. Keeps in the fridge for weeks.

Creamy Dressing

I use this dressing with coleslaws and potato salads. It is much lighter than using plain mayonnaise, and much nicer, too, I find!

Combine ¼ cup mayonnaise (I like to use Japanese mayonnaise), ¼ cup natural unsweetened thick Greek yoghurt, 2 teaspoons Dijon mustard and juice of ½ lemon. Makes about ½ cup. Keeps for a few days in the fridge.

Salsa Verde

This classic salsa is so useful and full of flavour. Even if you're not a fan of anchovies, I recommend you include them — once mixed in you can't tell they're in there and they add a wonderful depth of flavour. This salsa verde will liven up any meat, fish or chicken dish, or you can toss it through pasta or potatoes.

Combine ¾ cup very finely chopped flat-leaf parsley, 1 tablespoon very finely chopped fresh thyme, 1 tablespoon finely chopped capers, 1 minced clove garlic, 2 finely chopped anchovies, 2 tablespoons lemon juice, 1 teaspoon Dijon mustard and 3 tablespoons extra virgin olive oil. Season with salt and pepper. Makes about 1 cup. Keeps in fridge for up to a week.

Soy and Hoisin Dressing

This is an incredibly useful dressing for any Asian-style noodle dishes or salads. The hoisin adds a characteristic sweet and subtle spiciness.

Combine 3 tablespoons hoisin sauce, 1½ tablespoons sesame oil, 1½ tablespoons soy sauce and 1½ tablespoons rice vinegar. Makes about ½ cup. Keeps in the fridge for weeks.

Olive Tapenade

This is great spread on bread, served with an antipasto platter or in sandwiches.

Place 1¼ cups pitted kalamata olives and 3–4 tablespoons good-quality extra virgin olive oil in a food processor and blend until just combined. If you don't have a food processor, very finely chop olives and mix together with extra virgin olive oil. Makes about 1 cup. Keeps in the fridge for a couple of weeks.

Gremolata

A traditional Italian accompaniment, gremolata is full of fresh and zesty flavours and is great to serve with meat.

Combine 1 tablespoon finely chopped preserved lemon (alternatively use the finely grated zest of 1 lemon), 3 tablespoons finely chopped parsley, 1 minced clove garlic, 1 tablespoon lemon juice and 1 tablespoon extra virgin olive oil. Makes about ¼ cup.

Basic Sweet Chilli Dressing

Combine 2 tablespoons sweet chilli sauce, 3 tablespoons lemon or lime juice and 2 tablespoons extra virgin olive oil. Makes about ½ cup. Keeps in the fridge for a week.

Asian Sweet Chilli Dressing

Add 2 teaspoons fish sauce and 1 teaspoon sesame oil to the basic sweet chilli dressing. Makes about ½ cup. Keeps in the fridge for a week.

Honey Mustard Dressing

Combine 3 tablespoons red or white wine vinegar, 1½ tablespoons runny honey, 3 tablespoons extra virgin olive oil and 1 teaspoon wholegrain mustard. Makes about ½ cup. Keeps in the fridge for weeks.

Tandoori Seasoning

Great for marinating chicken.

Mix 3 teaspoons ground cumin, 2 teaspoons ground coriander, 1–2 teaspoons ground chilli powder, 2 teaspoons smoked paprika and 2 teaspoons ground turmeric together. Makes about ¼ cup. Keeps for months stored in an airtight container.

Harissa Paste

In a mortar and pestle, bash 3 cloves garlic, chopped, 1–2 red chillies, chopped, 1 teaspoon salt, 2 teaspoons cumin seeds and 2 teaspoons coriander seeds. Mix in ¼ cup olive oil and 3 tablespoons tomato paste. Alternatively, blitz all ingredients together in a food processor or blender. Fry paste in a hot pan until thickened, 4–5 minutes. Makes about ½ cup. Keeps in the fridge for up to a week.

Passionfruit Syrup

In a small pot, combine ½ cup passionfruit pulp (about 5–6 passionfruit) with 3 tablespoons sugar and juice of 1 lime. Boil gently for 5–6 minutes until thick and syrupy. Makes about ½ cup. Keeps in the fridge for a week.

acknowledgements

Massive thanks to Tam West for the stunning styling and photography. I'm very lucky to get to work with one super-talented lady with such a beautiful personality! It's always a pleasure and inspiration working with you (though it hardly feels like work).

Thanks, Carlos, Mum, Dad and the rest of the family for your continuing support and encouragement.

Thank you, Gideon Keith and Brittany Collard at Strategy Design and Advertising for the awesome design work and for turning my efforts into something I can be very proud of.

Thank you, Jenny Hellen, Tracey Lowndes and Rebecca Lal from Random House for producing this book — a lot of hours have gone in, so thank you all for your fantastic work; it's much appreciated.

I also have to say a special thanks to you everyday foodies out there who make my job a real joy — it makes my day to hear you're enjoying my recipes and, in particular, you're cooking more at home, eating more vegetables (especially the kids!), and feeling healthier. Keep up the good work!

index

A

apple
orange, beetroot & lemon
juice 36
slaw 170
spinach, carrot & orange
juice 36
apricot
chicken with mash, broccoli &
almonds 146
honey & orange blossom
yoghurt 28
Asian slaw 125
Asian sweet chilli dressing 253
asparagus
dill, caper & potatoes 98
fondant potatoes & cherry
tomatoes 141
olive panzanella 175
smoked salmon & avocado filo
baskets 84
autumn salad 169
avocado
& raspberry smoothie 30
mango & vanilla gelato 209
smoked chicken & mango
salad 46
smoked salmon & asparagus filo
baskets 84
smoky avocado, corn, capsicum
& egg potato salad 62
tartare 79

B

bacon & Brussels sprouts 166
baking *see also* bread; desserts
butternut cupcakes with cream
cheese icing & beetroot
sugar 239
dark chocolate, date & beetroot
cake 243
lime & coconut macaroons 231
little maple walnut cookies 240
mandarin syrup cake 198
mocha hazelnut layer cake 233
super breakfast muffins 18
balsamic glaze 75
banana
& pistachio cigars 205
choc-chip ice-cream 209
passionfruit, lime & coconut
sponge 247
barbecue prawns with spicy mango
& chilli dipping sauce 91
barbecued lamb & olive
panzanella 175
barley, roast butternut & lentil
peasant salad 116
basic sweet chilli dressing 46, 253
beans
fried tomatoes & celery 173
poached chicken, crouton &
green bean salad 59
roast tomatoes, spinach &
cannellini beans 176
smoked salmon Niçoise salad 63
Southeast Asian chicken &
potato curry 160
sundried tomato bean dip 68
beef
eggplant & ricotta lasagne 185
gourmet steak sandwich 193
Japanese beef & crunchy
vegetable soba noodles 65
open red wine beef pie with
baby vegetables 190
sizzling sherry & black pepper
beef hot plate 187
steak with orange miso sauce 194
tataki with apple & radish 83
beetroot
dark chocolate & date cake 243
mint & yoghurt dip 69
orange, apple & lemon juice 36
roast butternut, barley & lentil
peasant salad 116
thyme & goat's cheese tarts 119
venison & hazelnut salad 179

berries
avocado & raspberry smoothie 30
marinated 223
raspberry, strawberry &
cranberry juice 36
sauce 214
biscuits *see* baking
Black Doris plum sorbet 208
blue cheese, rocket & stone fruit
salad 169
bok choy 130
bread *see also* baking
croutons 59, 138
parmesan croutons 54
roast tomato, thyme & goat's
cheese crostini 75
sundried tomato, herb &
parmesan pizza bread 236
wholemeal kumara bread 235
breakfast
avocado & raspberry smoothie 30
chia seed pudding 38
creamy rice porridge 33
hash 'n' eggs 25
home-made yoghurt 28
juices 36
pita pockets 22
super breakfast muffins 18
tropical fruit muesli 21
vanilla & orange marinated
tamarillos 41
broccoli, kale, mushroom, tofu &
peanut noodles 103
broccolini
tomato, pine nut & parmesan
fettucine 120
with Chinese steamed fish 131
Brussels sprouts & bacon 166
bulgar wheat, grape, mint &
pine nut tabbouleh 145
butternut *see also* pumpkin
caramelised baby leek &
butternut pie 109
cupcakes with cream cheese
icing & beetroot sugar 239
satay soup 55

C

cabbage
apple slaw 170
Asian slaw 125
coleslaw 134
Japanese beef & crunchy
vegetable soba noodles 65
sesame cavolo nero 194
Cajun fish tacos with mango salsa
& chipotle sour cream 133
cakes *see* baking
capsicum
creamy roast capsicum soup
with parmesan croutons 54
smoky avocado, corn & egg
potato salad 62
caramelised baby leek &
butternut pie 109
caramelised onions 193
carrot
pineapple & ginger juice 36
roast butternut, barley & lentil
peasant salad 116
roast carrot, parsnip, herb & feta
Puy lentil salad 45
roast yams & carrots with
honey, coriander & dukkah 97
salad 189
spinach, apple & orange juice 36
cauliflower, roast cauliflower pearl
couscous 180
cavolo nero, sesame 194
celery
fried tomatoes & beans 173
potato & parsley salad 149
cheeses *see* particular cheeses
cherries with chocolate & red
wine syrup 220
chia seed pudding 38
chicken
apricot chicken with mash,
broccoli & almonds 146
harissa chicken with grape, mint
& pine nut tabbouleh 145
hot, sweet & smoky grilled
chicken 159
lemongrass & chilli lettuce cups 87
paprika chicken with tomatoes,
oregano & pine nuts 151
peanut, coriander & vermicelli
noodle salad 49
poached chicken, crouton &
bean salad 59
roast with Jerusalem artichokes,
bacon, Brussels sprouts &
gravy 166

roast with preserved lemon & date couscous & tahini yoghurt 156

schnitzel with potato, celery & parsley salad 149

smoked chicken, avocado & mango salad 46

Southeast Asian chicken, bean & potato curry 160

tandoori chicken skewers 162

Vietnamese noodle soup 165

chickpea
coriander hummus 68
tamari-roast pumpkin & walnut salad 60
tomato, spinach & paneer curry 104

chilled lemon soufflés 224

Chinese steamed fish parcels with coconut rice & broccolini 131

chipotle
pulled pork soft tacos with apple slaw 170
sour cream 133

chocolate
banana choc-chip ice-cream 209
cherries with chocolate & red wine syrup 220
dark chocolate, date & beetroot cake 243
mocha hazelnut layer cake 233

chorizo
Spanish fish stew 142
Spanish-style hash 'n' eggs 25

cinnamon crème fraîche 213

coconut
& lime macaroons 231
& mint sugar 202
lemon & almond pilaf 162
melon, honey & sago pudding 217
passionfruit, lime & banana sponge 247
prawn, watermelon & tamarind salad 56
rice 131
toasting 56
vanilla yoghurt panna cotta with marinated berries 223

coleslaw 134

confetti couscous 94

coriander
hummus 68
yoghurt 60

corn, smoky avocado, capsicum & egg potato salad 62

couscous
confetti 94
preserved lemon & date 156
roast cauliflower pearl couscous 180
summer 137

creamy
dressing 25
herb dressing 84
mango ice-blocks 219
rice porridge 33
roast capsicum soup with parmesan croutons 54
tarragon dressing 59

crisp baby vegetables 72

crispy-skin fish with Asian slaw 125

crunchy garlic potatoes 151

cucumber, basil & chilli mayo 76

cured salmon & avocado tartare 79

curries
chickpea, tomato, spinach & paneer curry 104
crushed potato with haloumi & poached egg 106
red duck & pineapple 158
Southeast Asian chicken, bean & potato 160

D

dark chocolate, date & beetroot cake 243

date, dark chocolate & beetroot cake 243

desserts see also baking; pies
banana choc-chip ice-cream 209
Black Doris plum sorbet 208
cherries with chocolate & red wine syrup 220
chia seed pudding 38
chilled lemon soufflés 224
coconut vanilla yoghurt panna cotta with marinated berries 223
creamy mango ice-blocks 219
feijoa & rhubarb almond crumble with ginger & brown sugar yoghurt 211
grilled peaches with berry sauce & pistachio crumble topping 214
grilled stone fruit with red wine syrup 218
kiwifruit & honey sorbet 208
mango, avocado & vanilla gelato 209
melon, honey & coconut sago pudding 217
pistachio & banana cigars 205
sticky red wine pears with cinnamon crème fraîche 213
tropical fruit carpaccio with mint & coconut sugar 202
Turkish rose pavlova 244
vanilla & orange marinated tamarillos 41

dill, caper & asparagus potatoes 98

dips
beetroot, mint & yoghurt 69
coriander hummus 68
mint & feta yoghurt 72
olive tapenade 141, 253
sundried tomato bean 68

dressings see also salads
Asian sweet chilli dressing 253
basic sweet chilli dressing 46, 253
creamy herb 84
creamy tarragon 59
cucumber & basil chilli mayo 76
gherkin 138
honey mustard dressing 253
lime & fish sauce dressing 125, 252
ponzu 78
red wine vinegar dressing 175, 252
soy & hoisin dressing 65, 103, 154, 252

drinks
avocado & raspberry smoothie 30
juices 36

duck
five-spice duck, pomegranate glaze, kumara mash & sesame spinach 153
red duck & pineapple curry 158
roast 154
shredded duck, orange & snow pea salad 154

E

eggplant
  beef & ricotta lasagne 185
  portobello mushroom &
    mozzarella free-form
    lasagne 113
  roast stuffed eggplant with
    Greek salad 110
eggs
  breakfast pita pockets 22
  chilled lemon soufflés 224
  curry crushed potato with
    haloumi & poached egg 106
  hash 'n' eggs 25
  huevos rancheros pita pockets 22
  smoked salmon Niçoise salad 63
  smoky avocado, corn, capsicum
    & potato salad 62
  Turkish rose pavlova 244

F

feijoa & rhubarb almond
  crumble with ginger & brown
    sugar yoghurt 211
fennel, autumn salad 169
feta
  mint & yoghurt dip 72
  roast carrot, parsnip & herb Puy
    lentil salad 45
fillings *see* icings, fillings & toppings
fish *see also* seafood
  Cajun fish tacos with mango salsa
    & chipotle sour cream 133
  Chinese steamed fish parcels 131
  crispy-skin fish with Asian
    slaw 125
  cured salmon & avocado tartare 79
  kokoda 92
  lemon, caper & parsley-crusted
    fish 137
  lime & basil cured salmon
    gravlax 88
  lime & sweet chilli glazed
    salmon 130
  pan-fried fish 138
  panko-crumbed fish 134
  salmon sashimi with ponzu 78
  salmon tom yum 126
  smoked salmon Niçoise salad 63
  smoked salmon, asparagus &
    avocado filo baskets 84
  Spanish fish stew 142
  Thai marinated fish carpaccio 80
  Thai salmon cakes 76
  with fondant potatoes,
    asparagus, cherry tomatoes &
    olive tapenade 141
five-spice duck, pomegranate
  glaze, kumara mash & sesame
  spinach 153

G

gelato *see* desserts
gherkin dressing 138
ginger
  & brown sugar yoghurt 211
  pineapple & carrot juice 36
glazed pork fillet, fried tomatoes,
  celery & beans with tasty
  rice 173
goat's cheese
  beetroot tart 119
  roast tomato & thyme crostini 75
gourmet steak sandwich
  with caramelised onions &
    horseradish crème fraîche 193
grape, mint & pine
  nut tabbouleh 145
gravy 166
Greek salad 110
green juice 36
gremolata 183, 253
  with ratatouille lamb 183
grilled peaches with berry sauce &
  pistachio crumble topping 214
grilled stone fruit with red wine
  syrup 218

H

haloumi, crushed potato &
  poached egg 106
ham, herb, spinach & egg pita
  pockets 22
harissa
  chicken with grape, mint & pine
    nut tabbouleh 145
  paste 145, 253
hash 'n' eggs 25
home-made yoghurt 28
honey
  kiwifruit sorbet 208
  mustard dressing 253
horseradish crème fraîche 193
hot Texas-style hash 'n' eggs 25
hot, sweet & smoky grilled chicken
  with salsa & coconut rice 159
huevos rancheros pita pockets 22

I

ice-cream *see* desserts
icings, fillings & toppings
  almond crumble topping 211
  chocolate icing 243
  cream cheese & banana
    filling 247
  cream cheese icing & beetroot
    sugar 239
  lime passionfruit curd 247
  mint & coconut sugar 202
  pistachio crumble topping 214

J

Japanese beef & crunchy
  vegetable soba noodles 65
Japanese rice 130
Jerusalem artichokes 166

K

kale, broccoli, mushroom, tofu &
  peanut noodles 103
kiwifruit & honey sorbet 208
kokoda 92
kumara
  chips 134
  mash 153, 194
  wholemeal kumara bread 235

L

lamb
  & tzatziki & roast cauliflower
    pearl couscous 180
  barbecued lamb & olive
    panzanella 175
  Lebanese pizza 189
  ratatouille with polenta &
    gremolata 183
  salsa verde lamb cutlets 176
Lebanese lamb pizza with carrot
  salad 189
leek, caramelised baby leek &
  butternut pie 109
lemon
  caper & parsley-crusted fish
    with summer couscous 137
  chilled lemon soufflés 224
  coconut & almond pilaf 162
  orange, apple & beetroot juice 36
lemongrass & chilli chicken lettuce
  cups 87
lentils
  roast butternut, barley & lentil
    peasant salad 116
  roast carrot, parsnip, herb & feta
    Puy lentil salad 45
lime
  & basil cured salmon gravlax 88
  & coconut macaroons 231
  & fish sauce dressing 125, 252
  & sweet chilli glazed salmon with
    Japanese rice & greens 130
  passionfruit, banana & coconut
    sponge 247
little maple walnut cookies 240

M

mandarin syrup cake 198
mango
  avocado & vanilla gelato 209
  creamy ice-blocks 219
  salsa 133
  smoked chicken & avocado
    salad 46
  spicy chilli dipping sauce 91
  tomato salsa 159
  tropical fruit carpaccio 202
melon, honey & coconut sago
  pudding 217
mint
  & coconut sugar 202
  & feta yoghurt dip 72
miso & orange sauce 194
mocha hazelnut layer cake 233
mozzarella, eggplant & portobello
  mushroom free-form
    lasagne 113
muesli, tropical fruit 21
mushroom
  broccoli, kale, tofu & peanut
    noodles 103
  eggplant, portobello mushroom
    & mozzarella free-form
    lasagne 113
  porcini mushroom, sage &
    spinach risotto 114

N

noodles
  broccoli, kale, mushroom, tofu
    & peanut 103
  Japanese beef & crunchy
    vegetable soba noodles 65
  peanut, coriander & chicken
    vermicelli noodle salad 49
  salmon tom yum 126
  Vietnamese chicken soup 165

O

olive tapenade 141, 253
  with fish 141
onions, caramelised 193
open red wine beef pie with baby
  vegetables 190
orange
  beetroot, apple & lemon juice 36
  miso sauce 194
  snow pea salad 154
  spinach, carrot & apple juice 36

P

pan-fried fish with crouton salad
& gherkin dressing **138**
paneer, chickpea, tomato &
spinach curry **104**
panko-crumbed fish 'n' kumara
chips with coleslaw **134**
papaya, tropical fruit carpaccio **202**
paprika chicken with tomatoes,
oregano & pine nuts & crunchy
garlic potatoes **151**
parmesan
croutons **54**
sundried tomato & herb pizza
bread **236**
tomato, broccolini & pine nut
fettucine **120**
parsnip, roast carrot, herb & feta
Puy lentil salad **45**
passionfruit
lime, banana & coconut
sponge **247**
syrup **231, 247, 253**
yoghurt **28**
pasta
beef, eggplant & ricotta
lasagne **185**
eggplant, portobello mushroom
& mozzarella free-form
lasagne **113**
sausage & three sisters penne
pasta **184**
tomato, broccolini, pine nut &
parmesan fettucine **120**
peaches, grilled with berry sauce &
pistachio crumble topping **214**
pear
& rocket salad **119**
sticky red wine pears with
cinnamon crème fraîche **213**
persimmon, autumn salad **169**
pies *see also* desserts
beetroot, thyme & goat's
cheese pies **119**
caramelised baby leek &
butternut pie **109**
open red wine beef pie with
baby vegetables **190**
smoked salmon, asparagus &
avocado filo baskets **84**
stone fruit tarts **201**
pineapple
carrot & ginger juice **36**
red duck curry **158**
tropical fruit carpaccio **202**

pistachio & banana cigars **205**
pizza
Lebanese lamb pizza **189**
sundried tomato, herb &
parmesan pizza bread **236**
plum
& cinnamon yoghurt **28**
Black Doris plum sorbet **208**
poached chicken, crouton & bean
salad **59**
polenta **183**
pomegranate glaze **153**
porcini mushroom, sage &
spinach risotto **114**
pork
chipotle pulled pork soft tacos
with apple slaw **170**
glazed fillet, fried tomato, celery
& beans **173**
thyme-crumbed chops **169**
potatoes
celery & parsley salad **149**
crunchy garlic **151**
curry crushed potato with
haloumi & poached egg **106**
dill, caper & asparagus **98**
fondant **141**
hash 'n' eggs **25**
mash **146**
salad **93**
smoked salmon Niçoise salad **63**
smoky avocado, corn, capsicum
& egg salad **62**
Southeast Asian chicken & bean
curry **160**
prawn, watermelon, tamarind &
coconut salad **56**
preserved lemon & date
couscous **156**
pumpkin
butternut cupcakes **239**
butternut satay soup **55**
caramelised baby leek &
butternut pie **109**
roast butternut, barley & lentil
peasant salad **116**
tamari-roast pumpkin, chickpea
& walnut salad **60**
purple juice **36**

R

ratatouille, lamb **183**
raw rainbow salad **50**
red duck & pineapple curry **158**
red wine
syrup **218**
vinegar dressing **175, 252**
rhubarb & feijoa almond
crumble with ginger & brown
sugar yoghurt **211**
rice
coconut **131, 159**
creamy porridge **33**
Japanese **130**
lemon, coconut & almond
pilaf **162**
porcini mushroom, sage &
spinach risotto **114**
tasty **173**
ricotta, eggplant & beef
lasagne **185**
roast
butternut, barley & lentil
peasant salad **116**
carrot, parsnip, herb & feta Puy
lentil salad **45**
chicken with preserved lemon &
date couscous & tahini
yoghurt **156**
chicken, Jerusalem artichokes,
bacon, Brussels sprouts &
gravy **166**
stuffed eggplant with Greek
salad **110**
tomato, thyme & goat's cheese
crostini **75**
tomatoes, spinach & cannellini
beans **176**
yams & carrots with honey,
coriander & dukkah **97**
rocket
stone fruit & blue cheese
salad **169**
rocket, pear salad **119**

S

sago, melon, honey & coconut
pudding **217**
salads *see also* vegetables
apple slaw **170**
Asian slaw **125**
autumn **169**
carrot **189**
coleslaw **134**
crouton **138**
grape, mint & pine nut
tabbouleh **145**
Greek **110**
olive panzanella **175**
orange & snow pea **154**
peanut, coriander & chicken
vermicelli noodle **49**
pear & rocket **119**
poached chicken, crouton &
bean **59**
potato **93**
potato, celery & parsley salad **149**
prawn, watermelon, tamarind &
coconut **56**
raw rainbow **50**
roast butternut, barley & lentil
peasant **116**
roast carrot, parsnip, herb & feta
Puy lentil **45**
smoked chicken, avocado &
mango salad **46**
smoked salmon Niçoise **63**
smoky avocado, corn, capsicum
& egg potato **62**
summer rocket, stone fruit &
blue cheese salad **169**
tamari-roast pumpkin, chickpea
& walnut **60**
venison, beetroot & hazelnut
salad **179**
salmon sashimi with ponzu **78**
salmon tom yum **126**
salsa *see also* sauces
salsa verde **176, 252**
salsa verde lamb cutlets with
roast tomatoes, spinach &
cannellini beans **176**
sauces
balsamic glaze **75**
berry **214**
chipotle sour cream **133**
chocolate & red wine syrup **220**
cinnamon crème fraîche **213**
coriander yoghurt **60**
ginger & brown sugar
yoghurt **211**

gravy **166**
gremolata **183, 253**
horseradish crème fraîche **193**
mandarin syrup **198**
mango salsa **133**
orange miso **194**
passionfruit syrup **28, 231, 253**
pomegranate glaze **153**
ratatouille **183**
red wine syrup **218**
salsa verde **176, 252**
spiced tomato **189**
spicy mango & chilli dipping
   sauce **91**
tahini yoghurt **156**
tomato **120**
tomato & mango salsa **159**
tzatziki **180**
sausage & three sisters penne
   pasta **184**
seafood *see also* fish
   barbecue prawns with spicy
      mango & chilli dipping
      sauce **91**
   prawn, watermelon, tamarind &
      coconut salad **56**
   smoky crayfish & potato salad **93**
shredded duck, orange & snow
   pea salad **154**
sizzling sherry & black pepper beef
   hot plate **187**
skewers, tandoori chicken **162**
smoked chicken, avocado &
   mango salad **46**
smoked salmon
   asparagus & avocado filo
      baskets **84**
   Niçoise salad **63**
smoky avocado, corn, capsicum &
   egg potato salad **62**
smoky crayfish & potato salad **93**
snow pea & orange salad **154**
sorbets *see* desserts
soups
   butternut satay soup **55**
   creamy roast capsicum soup
      with parmesan croutons **54**
   salmon tom yum **126**
   Vietnamese chicken noodle **165**
   Southeast Asian chicken, bean &
      potato curry **160**
soy & hoisin dressing **65, 103,**
   154, 252
Spanish fish stew **142**

Spanish-style hash 'n' eggs **25**
spice mixes
   harissa paste **145, 253**
   tandoori seasoning **162, 253**
spinach
   apple, carrot & orange juice **36**
   chickpea, tomato & paneer
      curry **104**
   ham, herb & egg pita pockets **22**
   porcini mushroom & sage
      risotto **114**
   roast tomatoes & cannellini
      beans **176**
   sesame **153**
steak with orange miso sauce,
   sesame cavolo nero & kumara
   mash **194**
sticky red wine pears with
   cinnamon crème fraîche **213**
stone fruit
   grilled stone fruit with red wine
      syrup **218**
   rocket & blue cheese salad **169**
   tarts **201**
summer couscous **137**
summer rocket, stone fruit & blue
   cheese salad **169**
sundried tomato
   bean dip **68**
   herb & parmesan pizza bread **236**
super breakfast muffins **18**
syrups *see* sauces

tacos
   Cajun fish **133**
   chipotle pulled pork **170**
tahini yoghurt **156**
tamari-roast pumpkin, chickpea &
   walnut salad **60**
tamarillo, vanilla & orange
   marinated **41**
tamarind water **56**
tandoori chicken skewers with
   lemon, coconut & almond
   pilaf **162**
tandoori seasoning **253**
tarts *see* pies
tasty rice **173**
Thai marinated fish carpaccio **80**
Thai salmon cakes with cucumber
   & basil chilli mayo **76**
thick red juice **36**
thyme-crumbed pork chops with
   autumn salad **169**
tofu, broccoli, kale, mushroom &
   peanut noodles **103**
tomato
   broccolini, pine nut & parmesan
      fettucine **120**
   chickpea, spinach & paneer
      curry **104**
   fried tomatoes, celery &
      beans **173**
   mango salsa **159**
   paprika chicken with tomatoes,
      oregano & pine nuts **151**
   roast tomato, thyme & goat's
      cheese crostini **75**
   roast tomatoes, spinach &
      cannellini beans **176**
   sauce **120**
   spiced sauce **189**
   sundried tomato bean dip **68**
   with fondant potatoes,
      asparagus, cherry
      tomatoes **141**
toppings *see* icings, fillings
   & toppings
tropical fruit
   carpaccio with mint & coconut
      sugar **202**
   muesli **21**
Turkish rose pavlova **244**
tzatziki **180**

vanilla & orange marinated
   tamarillos **41**
vegetables *see also* salads;
   particular vegetables
   baby **190**
   crisp baby vegetables **72**
venison, beetroot & hazelnut
   salad **179**
Vietnamese chicken noodle
   soup **165**

watermelon, prawn, tamarind &
   coconut salad **56**
wholemeal kumara bread **235**

yams, roast yams & carrots with
   honey, coriander & dukkah **97**
yellow juice **36**
yoghurt
   apricot, honey & orange
      blossom **28**
   beetroot & mint dip **69**
   coconut vanilla yoghurt panna
      cotta **223**
   coriander **60**
   ginger & brown sugar **211**
   home-made **28**
   mint & feta dip **72**
   passionfruit **28**
   plum & cinnamon **28**
   tahini **156**

T

V

W

Y